# Politics on the Inter

The Internet is revolutionising the way we live and interact with the world and is also changing the way we study. When it comes to politics we are faced with an immense volume of information which is often overwhelming, but properly harnessed can be inspiring and enlightening.

Today's students and scholars need new coherent strategies to approach their research and get the best out of information technology; with a clear, concise and focused structure, this book

- guides the reader to the best online politics sites and sources
- breaks the web down into manageable forms ideal for study
- deals with key issues such as plagiarism and newsgroups
- empowers study methods and builds confidence
- advises on how to get the best search results at speed

*Politics on the Internet* is a welcome gateway to the range of sources available; it opens up the best resource in contemporary politics and delivers the skills needed to master it.

This book will be of great interest to all students of politics and the media.

**Steve Buckler** is Senior Lecturer in the Department of Political Science at the University of Birmingham. His main research interests are in political theory and political ideology.

**David Dolowitz** is Reader in the School of Politics and Communication Studies at the University of Liverpool. His main research interests are in comparative public and social policy and in policy transfer between the United States and Britain.

# Politics on the Internet
A student guide

**Steve Buckler and David Dolowitz**

Routledge
Taylor & Francis Group

LONDON AND NEW YORK

First published 2005
by Routledge
2 Park Square, Milton Park, Abingdon, Oxon OX14 4RN

Simultaneously published in the USA and Canada
by Routledge
270 Madison Ave, New York, NY 10016

*Routledge is an imprint of the Taylor & Francis Group*

Typeset in Times by RefineCatch Ltd., Bungay, Suffolk
Printed and bound in Great Britain by
TJ International, Padstow, Cornwall

*British Library Cataloguing in Publication Data*
A catalogue record for this book is available from the British Library

*Library of Congress Cataloging in Publication Data*
A catalog record for this book has been requested

ISBN 0–415–26770–6 (hbk)
ISBN 0–415–26771–4 (pbk)

# Contents

# Illustrations

**Figures**

**Table**

**Box**

# Acknowledgement

The authors would like to express their thanks to Rebecca Eynon for her invaluable help in the production of this book.

# 1 Introduction

## The Internet – why bother?

> The highway is going to give us all access to seemingly unlimited
> information, any time, any place we care to use it. It's an exhilar-
> ating prospect, because putting this technology to use to improve
> education will lead to downstream benefits in every area of society.
> Bill Gates, *The Road Ahead*

Many people would be a little more sceptical than the world's
foremost software entrepreneur concerning the educational implications of the Internet. It is certainly true, however, that information technology will have a deep and continuing impact upon the
world of learning, as upon many other aspects of life; and, as a
student, you will find that the Internet inevitably plays a large part
in your studies. The increasing presence of computers and of
Internet access in homes and workplaces has been matched by
their prevalence in Higher Education. Computer technology has
become a basic aspect of provision for staff and students in universities and the use of the Internet for research and teaching is
now common. The purpose of this book is to provide a guide as
to how you might best and most effectively make use of the Internet in your studies. First, however, and since this is a book
designed specifically for *politics* students, it is appropriate to provide some sense of the politics of the Internet – of how it is used
politically and what the political impact of this new medium might
be. Equally, an awareness of the politics of the Internet may equip
you to ask some critical questions about the medium that will
prove important when you are actually using it.

**Where did the Internet come from?**

When investigating a particular phenomenon, political scientists will often be inclined to ask questions about where it came from and how it developed. It is instructive for us to look briefly at these questions in relation to the Internet. One frequently noted fact about computing technology is the speed with which it has become a major aspect of modern life. To quote just one of the many statistics, the number of computers in use in the United States alone increased from 5,000 in 1960 to 180 million by 1997.[1] A significant factor in this enormous increase has been the communications potential of computers once they are linked into networks. Computer networking emerged in fledgling form in the 1960s when the technology was developed that allowed information to be broken down into a form that was transmittable and readable by other machines. At this point, the potential range of networking was limited as the technology was developed and controlled by the US Defense Department. The ARPANET (Advanced Research Projects Agency Network), the precursor of the Internet, was developed in 1969 specifically for military and technical academic use. The widespread development of networking did not begin in earnest until the 1980s when the US National Science Foundation began to sponsor the linking up of computer systems between universities. More importantly perhaps, at this point, the intense lobbying that had been undertaken by the commercial sector throughout the 1970s and 1980s led to an increasing liberalisation of the data-processing industry. Companies began to develop their own corporate networks and these were linked up with increasing speed to form what, in the mid-1980s, became known as the Internet.

It was also at this time that some key developments occurred that were to turn the Internet into a publicly accessible and usable medium. Technology using HTML (Hypertext Mark-up Language) allowed graphic material to be displayed in documents; the development of the Domain Name System allowed easy identification of Internet sites and facilitated Internet searching; and the

---

1 Schiller 2000: 13

subsequent rise of commercial service providers allowed sub-scribers access to e-mail, web pages and user groups. With these developments, the Internet emerged as a site for information transfer and communication unprecedented in terms of access, range, volume and speed. This process culminated in a landmark ruling by the US Supreme Court in 1997 which removed all laws restricting the free flow of information on the Internet. This judgment set a worldwide precedent for liberalisation of online activity. When we look at its use in education as well as in other spheres, it is worth bearing in mind that although universities were amongst the first non-military users of the Internet, it is the commercial sector that has been central to the subsequent drive for more general access and usage.

Before we examine the specific uses of the Internet that you are likely to encounter in your studies, it is useful to add some further context, and raise some questions, by looking at the emergence of online technology in relation to politics.

## Politics and the Internet

There are two principal ways in which the Internet has come to figure politically. It is increasingly used by conventional political institutions, such as government agencies and political parties; but beyond this, Internet communication has made possible new forms of political organisation and interaction. Governments and political parties now routinely employ the Internet as a means of interacting with their constituencies through websites, e-mail and sometimes discussion forums. By these means they disseminate information and publicity, gauge opinion and engage in campaign activities. The Internet potentially has advantages for govern-ments or parties in that it provides a means of getting messages across whilst bypassing the kind of scrutiny and questioning that often accompany exposure in the traditional media. The flow of information may therefore be more easily controlled. The Internet also has the advantage of providing a cheap and immediate method of responding to events or of conveying messages. On the other hand, some in politics are less enthusiastic about the medium and see potential drawbacks. Perhaps the largest of these concerns the limited access to the Internet amongst the population as a whole: access remains most common amongst more advantaged social groups. As a result, key parts of the target audience remain unreachable in terms of online information or publicity. There is also a concern that the Internet represents a form of communication that is too passive and lacking in impact when compared with more traditional campaigning techniques. Perhaps because of concerns like this, the Internet has generally been regarded as simply a supplement to, rather than a replacement for, traditional modes of political communication. By the same token, it has tended, in traditional, mainstream politics, to be used in ways that reproduce traditional forms of communication and the potential that some would argue the technology contains for radically *new* forms of political interaction remains somewhat underexplored.

The question of how far the Internet could potentially change the political landscape is one that more frequently arises in the context of its use by groupings outside the framework of more traditional political institutions. This includes some groups that may have pre-existed the Internet but have been able to use it in order to expand or intensify their activity, and also groups that have been brought into being in virtue of the technology itself. Issue-orientated pressure groups, protest organisations and ideological movements outside the mainstream have made use of the Internet to extend their scope and their organisational focus in ways that traditional methods of communication did not permit. Equally, Internet user groups have sprung up which have created new spaces for e-mail-based political communication and debate, some at a relatively local level, others on a broader scale. The openness of the medium has in this way permitted users with common interests and concerns to discover one another and generate their own participatory forums.

The advantages of the technology in this respect lie in its global reach, the equal chances to participate in debate that it opens up and the level of interactivity that it offers. Some would also argue that the potential anonymity that comes with online communication is an advantage: exclusionary tendencies that come with recognition of class, race, gender and even accent are marginalised in the electronic forum. Factors of this sort have led some to regard the Internet as carrying profound implications for the future of political life. It has been argued that online political interaction will come to represent a new public sphere, accommodating an unprecedented diversity of voices and challenging the centralisation of the political process. Virtual political communities, it is suggested, will provide opportunities for direct participation that will revitalise political life at all levels. At more local levels, it may provide opportunities to integrate decision-making processes into communities themselves, generating new levels of 'social capital', the benefits accruing from interaction and mutuality. More broadly, the Internet may provide an interactive forum that will serve to reconfigure identities through cultural and political exchange and break down the stereotypes that underlie marginalisation. It may be that the Internet is still in its early stages as a political forum and still needs to develop values of civic engagement and real, deliberative communication, but the technology may hold considerable promise for the future.

Not everyone would share this optimism, however. Some would point to disadvantages inherent in the medium that potentially outweigh the advantages. Despite its global reach, the limitations on Internet access, especially in the developing world, make the political forum it offers much less inclusive (at least at present) than it initially might seem to be to those for whom the Internet is now a routine feature of life. And as we noted earlier, similar, if less pronounced, divisions also exist between different socioeconomic groups within the developed world itself. Also, online political debate is notorious for being, all too often, ill-informed, chaotic and lacking a proper deliberative element. Much interaction is in the form of unsupported assertion and is often uncivil. This would be enough to lead some to doubt that the anonymity afforded by online debate is necessarily a good thing, as it provides a context in which people do not feel the need to conduct themselves as responsibly as they would were they clearly identifiable. There may be other factors at work here as well. The lack of responsibility that characterises online interaction may reflect a lack of any sense of ownership of the medium, or any sense of control over the values embedded in it, on the part of most who use that medium. The design and development of the Internet have been driven by the application of technical expertise largely in the context of commercial interests: this may have created a sense of division between the professional owners of the medium and its generally passive users. It has been argued, in the light of this and the problems of differential access mentioned above, that the Internet, far from creating a transformed or revitalised public sphere, actually reproduces familiar inequalities and forms of exclusion. On this view, moreover, to the extent that the Internet does become an important feature of politics, it may serve to increase the opportunities for commercial interests to shape or dominate the political process.

Strong arguments may be made, then, both for and against the idea of the Internet as a potentially revolutionising and liberating political medium. Like most radically new technological phenomena, the Internet has tended to polarise opinion and it may be some time before it is possible to adjudicate with any certainty between the contending views here. What is not in doubt is that one way or another the Internet will be an important factor in politics as well as in many other areas of life. For students of politics, the kind of critical concerns raised here will be of continuing interest even as we use the medium itself as a research and learning tool.

## Learning and the Internet

Initially, in Higher Education, computer technology was deployed in specialist technical research but more lately it has become more deeply embedded in the sector's activities. As the capacity to place information on the Internet in a sophisticated and accessible form has developed, online research resources have become an important feature of academic life: bibliographical information, library catalogues, archives and databases of various sorts are all routinely used by academics. Equally, the Internet has facilitated networked collaboration and information sharing. The Internet has also itself become a site and object of research as it has developed into an important arena for social, economic and political interaction.

Since the mid-1990s, increasing access to the technology has meant that the Internet has come to feature much more prominently for students as well. Online resources can play an important role in your research. The Internet also provides a new way of accessing tailored information such as reading lists, course materials and research links. In addition, it is featuring increasingly in the learning and teaching process itself through the use of online teaching aids, e-mail discussion forums and Virtual Learning Environments (VLEs). With a new learning medium comes the requirement for new techniques for effective use and also new conventions for the integration of this medium into academic work as a whole. These are some of the issues with which this book is centrally concerned.

The following chapters will provide you with advice designed to help you become an efficient, and also a *discerning*, user of the Internet. This is an important issue in part because of the sheer openness of the Internet as a communications medium. Traditionally, certain criteria have operated that regulate the production and use of academic materials, through professional standards in publishing, copyright regulations, bibliographical cataloguing systems and so forth. These criteria are much more readily bypassed in the context of the Internet. The relatively easy and unregulated way in which information is published online, whilst in some ways a cause for celebration, might also prompt some caution when it comes to the use of such material in academic contexts. Discernment with respect to the origin and quality of the information that you find on the Internet is certainly called for.

A related issue here takes us back to the commercial forces that have played such an important part in fuelling and shaping the development of the Internet. Some would argue that this influence has resulted in a commercial orientation being built in to the 'virtual architecture' of the Internet. Commercial imperatives may have an influence upon the kinds of information provided and upon its mode of presentation. This potentially involves a 'commodification' of knowledge: commercial providers, for example, may be inclined to present information in a form that is most easily consumable by simplifying or sensationalising it. Information may also of course be presented in highly selective ways, and the principles of selection may need some examination. Equally, there may be a tendency to link web-based resources to further marketing opportunities: the line between information and advertising is one that may often quite easily become blurred. Another related development that has concerned some people in the USA in particular is the way in which the rise of networked educational provision has prompted alliances between universities, commercial content providers and technology companies. There are undoubtedly potential implications in this for the nature of Higher Education, as the interests of the commercial sector in more vocationally orientated study and training linked to research and development needs come to exercise more of an influence. The way in which use of the Internet in education might actually lead to a re-shaping of the educational agenda itself is a matter of ongoing concern. Again, in this context, a certain critical questioning of what is provided online is in order.

These are issues that you are likely to find prove relevant when you are researching on the Internet and when you come to make decisions about what information to use and how to use it. And with such issues in mind we will next go on, in chapter 2, to identify and categorise the many different kinds of resources available online that may be useful in your studies, including library resources, databases, media sources and many more. We will consider how to recognise different kinds of resources and how they may prove useful to you. Building on this, in chapter 3 we will consider how to make the most effective use of the Internet through appropriate search techniques. We will also look at the various types of subject directories and search engines that are available and how you can make the most use of them in your studies. Having looked at the important information sources and how to find them, in chapter 4 we will consider some guidelines you might follow that will help you be discerning with respect to the information you find via the Internet. We will consider ways in which you might assess Internet sites for probable accuracy and reliability and look at the places where you are most likely to find dependable sources. In chapter 5 we shall go on to look at how you might effectively use the Internet to conduct 'interactive' research – through the use of online questionnaires, discussions or focus groups. We will examine ways in which Internet technology facilitates this kind of research, which can prove very useful in the project work or dissertations that most students undertake at some point in their studies. In this chapter, continuing the interactive theme, we will also look briefly at learning on the Internet through the Virtual Learning Environments that are becoming an increasingly common feature of Higher Education. Throughout, the discussion will be illustrated with examples chosen to be of particular relevance to students of politics and international relations. We have also provided a general list of important Internet sites that are likely to be of use to you in your studies.

# 2 Resources on the Internet

When learning to use the Internet it is quite common for students to feel somewhat overwhelmed by the amount of information available. This can be a barrier to utilising the Internet as an effective research and learning tool. However, with a little understanding students can quickly learn how to utilise the Internet to its full potential. Not only can the Internet open the door to governments, think tanks, international organisations, databases, statistical information and media organisations, but it also allows students to contact individuals, groups and communities, while participating in online discussions, chats and events.

The primary purpose of this chapter is to help you find, recognise and understand the major categories of information available on the Internet and to indicate how these can be used to enhance the learning experience. Although one point should be made at the outset: no matter how much and what type of information is available online, the standard library is still, and will remain, a crucial resource in the learning process, for despite the hype surrounding the 'information super highway', the Internet is good for collecting some types of information but not so good for others. It is therefore a very useful supplement to the more traditional library-based research rather than a substitute for it. In general, for the foreseeable future, libraries are going to remain the best places to find books. While there are electronic books (e-books), these are limited and tend not to cover areas of interest to social science researchers and students (for some of the better sites for finding and accessing e-books, see: http://www.netlibrary.com; http://www.lib.utexas.edu/books/etext.html; http://gutenberg.lib.

md.us; http://info.lib.uh.edu/sepb/sepb.html; and http://www.ul.
cs.cmu.edu). Before going online or surfing the Internet, it is always
best to browse your library catalogue. A simple trawl though the
catalogue and associated book and journal stacks can provide a
wealth of information on your subject, as will a simple browse
through the table of contents and index of a selection of these
texts (for more information on the effective use of the library
prior to going online see: Rodrigues and Rodrigues 2000; Ó
Dochartaigh 2002).

Keeping in mind the continued importance of library research,
it is clear that the Internet is providing a new and expanding
source of information, capable of augmenting and enhancing the
information provided though more traditional sources. With this
in mind, before going online it is important to consider where the
information that you are interested in is likely to be available and
how it can be accessed most easily. In particular, the Internet is
becoming an increasingly useful source for: accessing up-to-date
information contained in databases and archives; finding documents published by governments, parties and interest groups; collecting data produced by a range of media outlets, academics and
organisations; finding and making contact with individuals,
groups and organisations; and conducing primary research, both
qualitative and quantitative. With this in mind, the remainder of
this chapter will consider:

- Databases and archives
- Government and party information
- Media sources
- Communication resources.

Of course, these classifications represent only one way of organis-
ing the data available on the Internet and information and data-
sets can and will overlap between different categories. However,
what follows aims to provide you with a good guide to understanding the types of data available and some of the ways to
utilise the data within the learning process.

Before we move to the specific categories, it is useful to understand some of the terminology associated with the Internet and so
it is worth now spending a paragraph on some technical jargon,

most of which you will probably already have encountered, even if you did not know its meaning. The most important point to remember is that while most people use the terms Internet and web interchangeably (in this book, we routinely use 'Internet' as the generic term) they are technically different. The Internet is a set of rules (or protocols) allowing interlinked yet independent computers and computer networks around the globe to connect and communicate. The World Wide Web (the web or WWW), on the other hand, is just one of the protocols used by the Internet. More specifically, the web refers to Internet sites using the Hypertext Transfer Protocol to communicate; you will probably be familiar with the 'http' designation in many addresses which indicates this. These sites contain files written in a specific computer language known as Hypertext Mark-up Language (HTML), designed to tell a web browser how to organise and display the information contained in the files. Each file (or page) has a unique Uniform Resource Locator (URL) address, the address that you need in order to call up those pages on your computer. However, while the web is the dominant part of the Internet, it is only one part. Other parts include sites utilising protocols such as e-mail (distributes electronic communications), File Transfer Protocol – FTP (transfers text or binary files between computers), Usenet (distributes information between newsgroups), and Telnet (allows the user to login and utilise a 'foreign' host computer). The point to remember is that while many of these protocols can be accessed using the latest versions of most web browsers (the two most popular being Netscape Navigator and Microsoft Internet Explorer), they are protocols that are independent of the web and as such can be used within computer mediated communications (CMCs) without recourse to web browsing software – itself nothing more than a program capable of reading and displaying web pages (for information on the structure and history of the Internet see: http://www.netvalley.com/netvalley/history-refer.html; http://www.lib.berkeley.edu/TeachingLib/Guides/Internet/WhatIs.html; http://www.isoc.org/internet/history; http://www.northernwebs.com/bc/.

A couple of further points are worth making before we move on to the specific categories of information. You should not lose sight of the fact that there is good, bad and outright deceitful information available on the Internet (a point to which we shall return in chapter 4). Nor should you become wedded to a particular search engine, source or type of information. With a little understanding, it is possible to recognise the different forms of information available online, how to use this information, and when particular types of resources are best used within the learning process.

## Databases and archives

Online databases and archives consist of materials that have been accumulated, stored and placed on the Internet either by individuals interested in a particular topic or, more often, by organisations of various sorts. Such archives may contain documents, images, audio recordings or other forms and combinations of electronic information. The advantage of the Internet here is that it allows these often unique collections of data to be easily located and searched by anyone having the basic skills and knowledge required to undertake a search. Importantly for the learning process, the information being placed into online databases is increasingly *only* being produced online and through that particular database, so the Internet in some cases becomes a unique source for the information you want.

Despite the wealth of up-to-date information contained in online databases, it is arguable that they are the most under-utilised, and least known, part of the Internet, because of the difficulty people sometimes experience in finding and accessing them. This is why databases and archives are sometimes referred to as the 'hidden' or 'invisible' web. However, once you become aware of, and capable of finding, the information contained in the databases and archives, these data-sets are likely to become one of the most important tools in the learning process. The reason for this is that the production, distribution and updating of Internet databases is fairly inexpensive in comparison with traditional means of publication, distribution and storage. As such, Internet databases allow individuals and organisations to provide substantially more information (both free and fee-based) to the public than has been possible previously. Equally, they expand the number of individuals and organisations who can access that information. As an electronic representation of data, they also make it possible to utilise the information in a variety of ways previously unavailable or available only at considerable expense. Take, for example, the US Census Bureau (http://www.census.gov). The statistical tables published by the Census Bureau can be downloaded directly into word-processing programs, such as Adobe Acrobat (PDF) files, or into almost any other data-processing programs, including Excel spreadsheets and math-ematical or statistical packages. All of this allows students and researchers to access and use far more data than has previously been available. This kind of data can prove useful at every stage of the research or study process, whether you use it as a starting point for developing a topic, or as a means by which to advance or focus the argument, or as evidence to be deployed in trying to defend the arguments you have made. For some of the better guides to finding social science databases, see: BUBL (http://bubl. ac.uk) and Search (http://search.com); for two of the best data-bases dedicated to general political science see: Keele University's Political Science Resource page (http://www.psr.keele.ac.uk); and the University of Michigan's Political Science Resource page (http://www.lib.umich.edu/govdocs/polisci.html).

### Online library resources

Beyond the general databases available to students of the social sciences the first, and in many ways the most important, set of databases the Internet makes widely available are those held by libraries. While most students have utilised the online catalogue of their own library to find books and journals, fewer know about or use the specialised databases offered by their libraries, and fewer still have used the Internet to access the databases and catalogues offered by 'foreign' libraries. Most university libraries are develop-ing and subscribing to a range of useful databases. While some of the more useful of these are only available to registered students, directly from library computer terminals, or though password connections, an increasing number are offering a range of services to the public. For instance, looking at the University of Liverpool's online catalogue, not only is it possible to search for the books, journals and special collections contained within the university's collection, but also to access a selection of other electronic databases. Looking at the databases offered under electronic resources (Figure 2.1), it is possible to access a range of journal/article databases directly from the library and the section relating to databases and CD-ROMs also allows anyone to access a range of databases displayed either alphabetically or by discipline. Not only do students have access to a range of databases to which the library subscribes, but as Figure 2.1 illustrates, students can also have access to databases containing information on other library catalogues, directories, search engines and skills packages.

Each of these resources can be utilised to help anyone at any stage of the learning process. For example, looking at the databases listed under 'Study Skills', they contain information and offer advice on a range of topics such as how to structure, research and write an essay as well as providing a link to the Univer-

*Figure 2.1* The University of Liverpool library page
[Reproduced with permission from the University of Liverpool library]

sity of Newcastle's database on Writing Research Theses and Dissertations. There is even information on how and where to get advice on finding employment.

While each university library site offers different information and directories, the point to remember is that that most are offering a wide range of databases which can be utilised to help both the research and learning processes of any student at any stage of their academic career. Thus, by taking some time to browse around, you are likely to discover much that is useful.

In addition to traditional libraries available, there are now also libraries that have been developed specifically for the Internet. These web-based electronic libraries are making a number of resources generally available which were previously known only to academics and professional researchers. An example of one of the best organised and user-friendly of these sites is the Internet Public Library (http://www.ipl.org). As can be seen in (Figure 2.2), IPL has been organised specifically to help students at every stage. For example, of particular use at the early stages of the learning process is the library's Reference Center, which includes general databases such as dictionaries, encyclopaedias and almanacs. It also includes information on writing skills. The IPL is not only useful at the initial stages of the learning process: once a basic understanding of a topic has been gained, students can use the subject-specific databases to find information directly related to their area of interest. A further feature of the IPL is its Pathfinder section. This has been developed specifically to help direct students at the early stages of their research by offering what the IPL staff consider to be the best starting databases and websites pertaining to a particular topic.

While all online libraries have a range of resources there are several worth mentioning specifically as they are universally accepted as amongst the most useful. The first of these is the British Library (http://www.bl.uk). Although it is not the easiest site to navigate, once you have found your way around you are able to view, reserve and order any of the library's own holdings. You can also make use of an extensive resource database for both the humanities and social sciences.

Another good example is the Library of Congress (http://www.loc.gov). This is the official library of the United States

*Figure 2.2* The Internet Public Library
[University of Michigan Board of Regents]

Congress, which professes to have the largest catalogue available
and has a number of useful databases and resources for students
of politics, including databases containing detailed information
on over seventy countries, databases covering a range of social
science disciplines, a database of national and international
libraries, links to other national governments and governmental
resources, and a paid research service.

You will also find Librarians' Index to the Internet (http://
lii.org) and the LibrarySpot (http://libraryspot.com) extremely
useful. As well as containing reference sections to help students at
the early stages of their research, these sites also have a number of
subject-specific links relevant to a broad range of political topics.
A final feature of LibrarySpot worth noting is its reading room,

which has a number of links to databases containing books, journals, newspapers and political speeches.

### *Journals*

While most libraries subscribe to a number of online journals – accessible though their catalogue or directly though a login name and password available from the library – if you are interested in a particular topic or author it is still necessary to discover what has been published and where, before taking advantage of the library's online journal resources. There are currently two key strategies for accessing this type of information. First, there are a number of online databases dedicated to indexing articles published in specific journals. Second, there are citation indexes which are databases compiled according to the citations of a journal article and its author/s. The first type is commonly available though the online resources offered by most libraries. Thus, looking back to the University of Liverpool, by accessing the electronic resources page and going to the database and CD-ROM section, you can find a number of social science resources, including several databases of journal articles, searchable by author, title, date or keywords.

For social scientists and students of politics in particular, there are several key citation databases worth knowing about. These are archives that record publications by reference to citations in other works. One example is to be found at the web of knowledge (http://wok.mimas.ac.uk). Students at any college or university will have access to the WOK databases through their institution, via a personal account and password. Once inside the Web of Knowledge the most relevant portion will be the Social Science Citation Index (SSCI), which is a database of thousands of articles cited in hundreds of journals, going back to the early 1990s. This database can be used to discover what has been published in a particular area and also, as an index compiled though citations, to trace the academic literature on a particular topic by following the citation links.

In addition to the SSCI, students will find JSTOR (http://www.jstor.org) just as useful, even though it has a considerably more limited database. As with the WOK, students at any college or university will have access to the JSTOR databases through their institution, via a personal account and password. Unlike the Social Science Citation Index, JSTOR has full text copyright (PDF) for articles published in a range of journals. However, rather then being indexed based on citation, JSTOR indexes every article found in its journal database. A particularly useful feature of the JSTOR database is that it can be searched by category or by individual journal so that the range of returns can be limited to very specific subjects and articles. Whilst a little dated, the Directory of Electronic Journals and Newsletters (http://www.arl.org/scomm/edir), is another useful site which has links to over 16,000 web-based sources. Similarly, the Electronic Journal Miner (http://ejournal.coalliance.org) offers a fairly useful resource for finding both peer and non-peer reviewed academic publications.

Two further services worth mentioning are Northern Light (http://www.northernlight.com) and LexisNexis (http://www.lexisnexis.com). While both of these are commercial sites, they are useful for students interested in a journalistic approach to their research, in looking at how the media portrays given issues, or in using newspapers and magazines in their studies. Both are known for their comprehensive database of newspaper and magazine articles. However, as a commercial site Northern Light charges a fee for each article ordered and as a general rule the only feasible way to utilise LexisNexis is if your university or college subscribes to the service (if your institution does subscribe to LexisNexis you will find it available via the library's online catalogue and a login name and password should be available for students working outside the library).

### *Document delivery services*

One of the less well-known areas of the Internet is the growing number of document delivery services. These sites are dedicated to finding and photocopying articles on request. While all of these sites charge for their services most of the cost goes to covering the copyright fee, or searching for those extremely obscure articles which are almost impossible to find. As an example, one of the more established services is IngentaConnect (http://www.ingentaconnect.com), which has a searchable database and will deliver documents via fax or e-mail. To get a fuller idea of what is available it is worth a look at the Association of Independent Information Professionals (http://www.aiip.org). This site has been developed for 'professional' information delivery companies and as such gives you an idea about what types of services actually available for payment. It also has a directory, which can be utilised to find members that are dedicated to document delivery.

### Online bookstores

For students interested in finding out what books are available or who want to purchase a text there are a number of excellent online bookstores. The most popular and well publicised of these is Amazon (www.amazon.co.uk or http://www.amazon.com). There are other sites which are particularly useful for finding out-of-print material, such as Powell's online service (http://www.powells.com). For students interested in exploring what type of information has been published or is scheduled for publication, relating to their topic there are few better sites than Booksinprint (http://www.booksinprint.com). This has one of the most complete catalogues of books currently in print or scheduled for publication and also a good out-of-print locator service.

### Statistics and data archives

Not only are a variety of libraries available online but the Internet has opened up the world of statistics and data archives to any student wishing to explore these areas. The use of computers to store and analyse statistical data has been common in the social sciences since the early days of the computer revolution. Before the advent of the Internet, much of the data contained in these databases was only available to the institution responsible for the data or to researchers willing to visit the institution where the data was stored. With the development of the Internet, however, many of these databases are now opening themselves up to the wider public. Leading this trend are governments and universities who are increasingly using the Internet to make available tables of pre-analysed data and to provide raw data-sets which can be analysed by the individual researcher to fit their purpose using a number of different statistical programmes. Progressively more institutions are publishing data that can be displayed in a number of different combinations directly from their websites (for all three on one site see: http://www.opensecrets.org).

While there are vast numbers of institutions publishing useable data online, there are a few specifically recognised for their quality and usefulness to students of politics and international relations. One of the best examples in this area is the University of Michigan Document Center (http://www.lib.umich.edu/govdocs/polisci. html). This site is one of the largest, best-designed guides to all sorts of political science data. Organised by broad subject categories covering all areas of politics and the learning process it also has a site to dedicated social and political statistics which leads students to thousands of sites containing data on almost any subject. Another good example of a statistical clearing site is the UK National Statistics website (http://www.statistics.gov.uk). This site provides a collection of statistics, reflecting the state of the British economy, population and society. Also, FedStats (http://www.fedstats.gov) offers a gateway to the entire collection of statistics published by the US government. As can be seen in Figure 2.3, one of the better features of this site is that it simplifies the search process by allowing information to be accessed either by topic, agency or subject. It also includes links to useful statistical sources outside the government.

In addition to the institutions publishing statistical information directly on the Internet there are a large number of organisations who store data-sets compiled by a range of organisations. As these sites begin opening their databases to the public a huge resource of quantitative and qualitative data is becoming available to those who know how to access the information. A good example of this is the Essex Data Archive (http://www.data-archive.ac.uk). The Essex Archive contains a large number of data-sets compiled by government-funded projects and academic studies. It also offers links to other archives thoughout the world, many of which are available to UK-based students through the Essex Archives reciprocal agreements.

Two further examples worth mentioning, both for what they contain and for their links to other archives, are the Council of

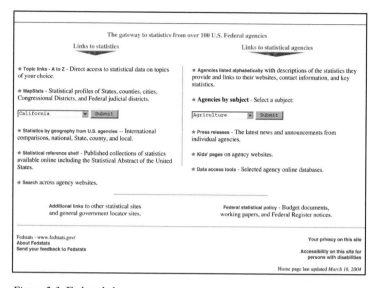

*Figure 2.3*  Fedstat's home page
[Fedstats, Interagency Council on Statistical Policy, Office of Management and Budget, Washington DC, 2004]

European Social Science Data Archives (CESSDA) (http://www. nsd.uib.no/cessda) and the National Digital Archive of Datasets (NDAD) (http://ndad.ulcc.ac.uk). Both of these archives contain data useful to students of politics and can be accessed free of charge.

## Government and party information

Over the past decade some of the most comprehensive and advanced sources of information on the Internet have emerged from local, regional and national governments and intergovernmental organisations (IGOs). Not only are governments and IGOs publishing a range of statistics on the web, but they are also publishing a vast array of documents, pamphlets, studies, reports, records of hearings and other official meetings, and an array of rulings – some of which are being released exclusively online. In view of this, one of the core skills any student interested in politics should learn is how to find and utilise this sort of information.

This requires a little application because, as a general rule, few search engines can access all of information being published by governments and those that are capable of accessing some of the information do not tend to organise it efficiently into usable packages. Thus, it will only be by discovering and using a range of specialised resources that you will be able to access the information being produced by governments and IGOs in a fast, efficient and reliable manner.

The United States local, state and federal governments are at the forefront of Internet-based information releases and provide some good examples of what is available. At the apex sits the federal government and its various executive and congressional agencies. All of these institutions have an online presence which can be accessed either directly or though specialised search resources. Some of the best ways to begin finding the resources provided by local, state and national government in the United States are: FedWorld (http://www.fedworld.gov), the Federal Web Locator (http://www.infoctr.edu/fwl), the Library of Congress's Government Resources site (http://lcweb.loc.gov/rr/news/extgovd.html), State and Local Government on the Net (http://www.statelocalgov.net) and the Pew Research Center (http://www.stateline.org).

There are many websites taking students directly to individual government pages and databases cataloguing the governments of the world. Two good examples of starting points for entering this almost limitless area of research are the Government Online Resource site (http://library.uww.edu/subject/govinfo.htm) and University of Michigan's Foreign Government Document Center (http://www.lib.umich.edu/govdocs/frames/forfr.html). In addition, Governments on the WWW (http://www.gksoft.com/govt) and BUBL's national government home page (http://www.bubl.ac.uk/link/n/nationalgovernments.htm) provide comprehensive databases covering a range of national governments and the resources being provided by these governments. In terms specifically of British politics, it is worth noting that the UK government has recently launched itself onto the Internet through a single gateway called DirectGov (http://www.direct.gov.uk), which aims to become as comprehensive as similar gateways found in the United States.

Intergovernmental Organisations are also increasingly placing information on the Internet. Whilst many politics students will be aware of the United Nations website (http://www. unsystem. org) and the European Union's home page (http:// www.europa.eu.int), almost every IGO has its own website. Accessing and making use of the fullest range of these sites takes some browsing around but help is at hand in the form of sites offering useful portals by which to enter this area. Two good examples are the University of Michigan's Document Center (http://www.lib.umich.edu/govdocs/intl.html) and Northwestern's International Governmental Organisation Publication Resource site http://(www.library.northwestern.edu/govpub/resource/internat/igo.html).

## Media sources

As the Internet develops, it is simultaneously altering the way individuals receive and use the media. The web has allowed thousands of newspapers, magazines, network TV and radio stations, and even interest groups to disseminate conventional and alternative interpretations of political events electronically. This allows individuals to cull numerous sources and interpretations of political events quickly and efficiently. In fact, once you have a basic knowledge of how the media is represented on the Internet, you can receive information on almost any political event, and almost any political or ideological interpretation, as the event occurs or by looking though archived information.

### *TV and radio: the news*

Clearly the most recognisable sources of news on the Internet are online versions of conventional TV news broadcasts. While most of these sites look much like magazines, they in fact offer services ranging from online versions of their regular broadcast programmes to specialised search facilities and 'in-depth' coverage of major current events. While almost every major television station has a presence on the Internet, three of the best starting points for mainstream news coverage are: the BBC online (http://www. bbc.co.uk), which offers a range of services, including access to the World Service, radio programmes, and a search facility that can be limited to BBC news stories; CNN International (http://www.cnn.com), which provides access to its Headline News service, is available in multiple languages and has links to other news sources; and MSNBC (http://www.msnbc.com), which is a joint venture between Microsoft and the NBC television network.

Many radio stations also now place news online. These stations not only provide sources of news and information, but many also offer supplementary services ranging from transcripts of public proceedings to in-depth analysis of major events. While there are thousands of web-based radio stations, it is not necessarily that easy to find stations dedicated to providing news coverage. Two good portals for finding a range of sites dedicated to the news are (http://www.newspapers.com/tv_radio.htm) and (http://www.rlbecker.com/news.htm). Both of these sites provide access to global 24-hour news stations, including a variety of stations providing 'alternative' interpretations of current events and events not discussed in the mainstream press. Two good examples of radio station sites are, in Britain, the BBC online radio services, and in America, National Public Radio (http://www.npr.org), which can be accessed via their home pages.

### *Online newspapers*

Probably the most extensive source of online news is available though electronic newspapers. Given that there are thousands of these, the first task any student needs to perform when using electronic newspapers in their studies is to determine the most appropriate kind of source for their purpose. Thus, if you are interested in American politics it is probably best to access an American newspaper; similarly if you are interested understanding how the Arab world views events in the Middle East you can access newspapers being produced in the Arab world. This task is made easier by various portals dedicated to cataloguing newspapers and directing you to the appropriate sources. A good example here is the Ultimate Collection on NewsLink (http://newslink.org). This is a collection of newspapers from around the world, organised by region and country, which also has links to radio and television stations providing news coverage in the selected country and region. Some other useful sites of this sort are Newspapers Online (http://www.newspapers.com), News Directory (http://ecola.com) and, My Virtual Newspaper (http://www.refdesk.com/paper.html). All of these sites provide excellent portals to the world press. A final engine worth looking at is the Alternative Press Center (http://www.altpress.org), which offers the best portal for finding and reading newspapers and articles offering alternative interpretation of current events and issues.

### Online news magazines

There are a number of online news magazines emerging dedicated to particular topics that might interest the social scientist. However, as with newspapers, the key to entering the world of e-zines is to find a portal capable of guiding you though the thousands of online magazines that exist. In this area, ListFish (http://www.listfish.com) and the Ezine Directory (http://www.ezine-dir.com) are good examples, particularly with regard to their news and politics selections. For those looking for a specific topic or specialised information there are also very good e-zine search facilities available, including FindArticles (http://www.findarticles.com) and Northern Light (http://www.northernlight.com).

### News services

The Internet also offers a way of collecting snippets of information from all the sources listed above by going to newsgathering services. There are websites dedicated to gathering news headlines from around the world and remove the need to spend hours surfing the web looking for news related to your topic. A good example is News Now (http://www.newsnow.co.uk/). This site claims to be monitoring over 7,000 news sources every 5 minutes, making it one of the most up-to-date information sources available on the web. Similar sites can also be found at News Is Free (http://www.newsisfree.com) and ABYZ (http://abyznewslinks.com). A very useful feature that these sites offer is the ability to limit the news items returned to specific topics. Picking up on this idea, those interested in following the coverage of a particular topic or subject by the world media can use sites such as Pandia (http://www.pandia.com/news/), Moreover (http://w.moreover.com), and 1st Headlines (http://www.1stheadlines.com). These sites search a wide range of sources for breaking news and allow users to search their catalogues by news category and keyword.

### *Weblogs and webrings*

For students interested in researching a particular subject, weblogs (or blogs) and webrings are overlooked resources. A weblog is a site developed by an individual which is regularly updated and which reflects the particular interests and experiences of that individual. Sometimes these can be very useful in exploring a particular subject. A good example is the weblog kept by the so-called 'Baghdad Blogger' during and after the Iraq War. This weblog provided a unique insight into events as they were experienced by ordinary citizens in Iraq. There are hundreds of weblogs available and two sites that will help you find them are the Guardian Unlimited (http://www.guardian.co.uk/weblog), and Yahoo's guide to politics weblogs (http://uk.dir.yahoo.com/Computers_and_Internet/Internet/World_Wide_Web/Weblogs/politics/).

Like weblogs, webrings bring together a series of resources dedicated to a specific subject or similar subjects. However, unlike blogs, webrings are a series of web pages linked together. Thus, instead of having a single site directing you to other sites and resources, webrings are linked sites designed to direct you from one on to the next, as if you had entered large circle of sites. Thus, by accessing a webring you will be able to focus on a selection of sites dedicated to a given subject without having to worry about surfing into unrelated areas. Two sites which can help direct you to the world of webrings are Webring (http://www.webring.com) and RingSurf (http://www.ringsurf.com).

### Communication resources

One of the most useful aspects of the Internet for the learning process is the increased opportunities it affords for students to communicate with one another and with the wider academic community. The Internet makes it possible for you to find people interested in the same questions as you are, to contact experts and discuss what they know about a topic of interest, to get involved in group discussions relating to your area of interest, and even to receive regular updates directly to your e-mail system relating to almost any topic of interest. The primary (although not the only) tools in this ever-widening world of Internet communications consist of: e-mail, listservs (also referred to as listservers and mailing lists) and Usenet (also known as newsgroups). These methods of communication will be examined in terms specifically of their use in 'interactive research' in a later chapter, but they are worth mentioning briefly here as general sources of information.

### *E-mail*

The most used feature of the Internet is electronic mail (e-mail). While most students routinely use e-mail to contact friends and family it is now increasingly being employed to make contact with academics and experts working in a given area of research, to conduct interviews and surveys, to check facts and figures, as a means of receiving updates, press releases and alerts. As most of you will have discovered, not only can e-mail be used to send and receive messages but most programs allow you to add and open attachments – files prepared by another program and then added to an e-mail message. You can utilise this in your learning process to augment an assignment by e-mailing a survey to an expert, a newsgroup, or even your classmates.

Additionally, a secondary form of e-mailing, called instant messaging, is becoming an increasingly popular means of communicating over the Internet. This program (available from AOL http://www.aol.com; MSN http://messenger.msn.com; and Yahoo http://messsenger.yahoo.com), has been developed to let you conduct real-time conversations with other people or groups using the same software program. As should be clear, having the ability to 'talk' to people instantaneously over the Internet opens a range of creative learning possibilities. Not only can the technology be used to help in group work, where students can readily talk to each other, but interviews can also now be conducted quickly and without the delays which one can sometimes experience when conducting traditional in e-mail interviews or surveys.

### *Listservs (mailing lists)*

Listservs (or listservers) are online discussions groups where communication takes place through group e-mail communications. We will discuss how to find listservs in chapter 3, but it is worth noting that, as there are thousands of listservs covering thousands of topics, they can be a very good resource for finding experts and expert information in almost any area you might be interested in studying. Once you join a mailing list (you must subscribe to a mailing list to receive its postings) the information posted by other members is sent directly to your e-mail account and any information you post to the routing computer will be sent to the e-mail accounts of all other individuals signed up to the mailing list. In the learning process, listservs are a good way to find information, keep up to date, and in some cases be posted of any major announcement or event relevant to your listserver. For example, anyone interested in activities of the US Government Accounting Office can sign-up to the GAO's listserver (http://www.gao.gov), while anyone interested receiving press notices from the HM Treasury (UK) can sign up for these by sending an e-mail to: presslist@hm-treasury.gov.uk.

Finally, it is worth remembering when signing up to listservs that they do not all operate in the same way. Some operate two-way communications, where members can send messages to the server which will route the message to others on the list, while other servers only allow their operator to send messages out to members. As a rough and ready guide, most of the listservs operated by government and media agencies are of the latter sort while most academic, group and specialist listservs are of the former.

### *Usenet (newsgroups)*

In addition to listservs, you can get involved in discussions relevant to your interests by following or joining the discussions of newsgroups. In brief, Usenet refers to a network of computer discussion groups that can be accessed and joined by anyone online, without having to sign up formally for the group.

Officially, a newsgroup does not have to have anything to do with the news (though any given group might be discussing current events). Rather, a newsgroup is an online discussion of a particular topic that anyone can join. It is advisable, before actively joining a conversation, to 'lurk' on the site without participating to see what kind of group it is. Some groups can turn out to be unpleasant, being given over more to invective than to any genuine discussion or exchange of information. Clearly, you will not want to waste your time with groups of this kind. If you decide that the group is legitimate and you want to ask it a question relating to your studies, consider looking though the group's frequently asked questions (FAQ) file because some group members can get irritated with those who ask questions that the group have already dealt with or have been listed in the FAQ section. Finally, always consider how you ask your questions or respond to other members. Being adversarial or offensive can often lead to a 'flame war', where things become personal and communication antagonistic. This clearly reduces the usefulness of the group, sometimes leading to its abandonment, or to your removal from any further group discussions.

While there are no codified rules governing behaviour online, a set of norms has been emerging which are generally regarded as the appropriate rules of 'netiquette' – the table below is a compilation of the most commonly recognised elements. If you are interested in learning more about the norms of online behaviour see: Shea 1994; http://www.albion.com/netiquette; http://www.learnthenet.com/english/html/09netiqt.htm

There is one final point that you should remember in terms of Internet communication. Anything you might post on the Internet is available for anyone to read or to cut and paste into any other document or programme, and, further, it will generally *remain* available until you actively remove it. This is true whether you are using e-mail or simply posting a message to a listserv group. As such, it is advisable to act online as you would in any public context and where what you do or say could be recorded for posterity.

---

**Box 2.1 Ten tips for Internet communications**

While there are no set rules governing online interaction and different forums require slightly different types of behaviour as a general rule there are ten key tips anyone wanting to engage in Internet communications should consider.

- At the outset tell your reader exactly what the purpose of your message is and what information you are looking for
- Always disclose your true identity and let the readers know what purpose you have for your communications
- If using listservs do not post a question before searching the site's FAQ section
- Do not post messages or ask questions which are inappropriate for the group or individual you are making contact with
- Choose your wording carefully! It is easy to misinterpret online communications

- Lurk before you leap! It is always best to get a feeling of a site or group before you begin engaging in Internet communications
- Never ask for information that is easily available elsewhere on or off the Net
- Always reread your messages before sending them to ensure you have the correct tone, spelling, grammar, etc.
- Do not expect people to respond immediately to your messages, whether sent via e-mail or posted to a group
- Always treat those online as you would like them to treat you

---

## Conclusion

There is an almost limitless range of resources available though the Internet to help enhance your knowledge and learning efforts. This chapter has been designed to help you organise this vast array of information into useable categories. While there is clear overlap between the categories developed, by following them you should be able to understand the various sites you are going to encounter on the Internet. Next we shall consider how to find these resources through efficient searching on the Internet.

# 3 Using the Internet

Chapter 2 catalogued a variety of online resources you can utilise throughout your learning lifetime. This will have given you a sense of the sheer volume of information that is available on the Internet. Whilst it is clearly one of the strengths of the Internet that it is possible to enquire into almost any subject that you might be interested in, this wealth of information is also arguably a potential weakness. With over two billion publicly accessible web pages, tens of thousands of experts operating online, and millions of non-web-based resources available though the wider Internet, finding the information you really need can be difficult. However, there are some very useful ways in which you can influence the number and type of returns, or 'hits', you encounter when conducting Internet research. Thus, while the Internet is like an ocean and many people use it to surf from site to site, this chapter will help you learn how to turn the ocean into a pond that contains material of direct relevance to your interests. It will introduce you to the world of general, meta and specialised search engines and subject directories and will consider how you can make the best use of these tools. As part of this, we will also examine the structure of Internet addresses and endings to show you how it is often possible to guess the address of a site where you can find the information you are looking for without having to spend time utilising a search tool.

## Developing a search strategy

There are a number of tools available to sift though the vast amount of information available online, but to maximise the usefulness of these tools it is advisable first to develop a strategy capable of focusing your online searches on the tools you require. This will help you maximise the likelihood of finding the information you desire and if you are unsuccessful in your first search, you can easily move to a second approach and will not waste time.

In order to maximise the potential of the Internet to complement your learning, it is necessary sometimes to avoid many of your first instincts: do not always head straight to your favourite search engine (i.e. the one you have been using since you first went online) and do not type in the first word or phrase that comes to mind. This may often get you thousands of hits and it will probably take you longer to sift though the material in an effort to find useful information than if you slowed down and developed a simple search strategy. A good strategy to adopt is to ask yourself three questions before even turning on your computer: What am I looking for? Where am I most likely to find it? What are the most relevant search terms for my purpose?

### *What am I looking for?*

When you have a general topic or assignment that you think might benefit from online research the best thing you can do first is to spend time thinking about what it is specifically that you need to research. The best way to begin here is to express the information you are interested in finding in a sentence or two. This will allow you not only to narrow your search to but it will also help you focus in on the type of information your are looking for (person, event, place, time, . . .), the types of words and phrases associated with your topic, and the tools you might need to utilise in your search (people finders, specialised search engines, topic specific databases, . . .). For example, if your topic is about federalism in the expanding European Union, you might formulate some of the following types of questions:

- What are the key issues surrounding federalism and how will these help me gain a greater understanding of the current debates occurring in the media?

- What is there to know about the history of American federalism and how can this help my understanding of how the European Union operates?
- What are the philosophical roots of federalism and how do these debates help my understanding of the debates surrounding the dangers of a federal Europe.

Specifying questions in this way will help focus your search and is a much better way to start than simply typing 'Europe' into a search engine, producing a large number of sites most of which will probably be irrelevant.

### What are the most relevant search terms?

Once you have enough information on your topic to determine the question/s you are interested in pursuing, you should then consider the types of concepts that are contained within your question and any possible synonyms, keywords or phrases that might be useful in narrowing the number of hits you receive once commencing your online search. Going back to the topic of federalism, if you are interested in researching the issues associated with the first question you might think of some of the following terms: devolution, subsidiarity, federalism, intergovernmental relations. Considering the second, you could also look for phrases such as: 'history of American federal state relations', 'relations between states', 'types of governance in the United States', and 'distribution of power within the United States'. Or you might try phrases such as: 'what is federalism?' or 'conceptions of federalism'.

As part of this process, it is also important to consider just what type of information you are looking for. For example, if you are looking for statistics on the number of nations organised along federal lines or how many sub-governments exist within Europe or the United States, you will need to search very different sources from those required if you are looking for the philosophical origins of the concept of federalism or even if you are looking for information on the major arguments in support of federalism.

### *What's the best search tool for my enquiry?*

Regardless of the question you ask or the terms and phrases you consider important, you are still going to have to use this information to identify the types of search tools that will best match your needs. As we shall see below, there are a variety of tools available to help you find information on the Internet, each with its own advantages and disadvantages. Few of the problems generally encountered here have to do with the inherent characteristics of that tool. Rather, most shortcomings of online searches result from the wrong tool being used. For example, if you do not know much about a topic it is always better to start with a directory than an engine (we will look at these tools in more detail alter on). Similarly, if you are looking for the answer to a very specific problem, and you are fairly certain of how to phrase your search parameters, you will probably be better off going to a search engine.

## Search techniques

Unlike traditional libraries or archives, the Internet does not have any single universal index to the information it contains, so it is not always easy to find the specific information you are looking for online. Because of this, search tools have become one of the Internet's most useful elements. However, it is important to understand not only how search tools operate but also the differences between them, for depending on the tool you use, the same search will generally return substantially different results. In fact, even different versions of the same tool (e.g. the search engines Google and Alta Vista) will return different results. At a general level the two most common search tools are *search engines* and *subject directories*. We shall look at these in more detail shortly but first it is worth noting that there are other ways of accessing sites on the Internet. Of these, probably the most underutilised technique consists simply in using an educated guess to enter a site's address directly into your chosen browser.

### The address

In order to utilise web addresses effectively, it is worth taking a few minutes to familiarise yourself with the core components contained in every web address. The key here is every site's exclusive Uniform Resource Locator (URL) address. These addresses are unique mixtures of letters and numbers that identify the computers, directories, folders, and/or files that contain the information you are looking for. This holds true no matter where you go or what you access online, and so one of the keys to understanding the Internet is to understand the structure of URL addresses. Once you know a little about the structure of these addresses, you should be able to make educated guesses as to the address of the site you are interested in and also to identify and work out the type of organisation that has produced or published online the information you access. You will also have a better idea of how to expand your search of a site, how to see if there is more relevant information available, or, when you get an error message, how to find out if the information you are looking for has been moved to another location on the server. You should even be able to identify any entry errors in the information appearing in an address that might be leading to error messages.

Taking Figure 3.1, you can see that this fictitious URL is composed of four key components, the protocol, the domain name, directories/folders, and a specific file.[1] Everything appearing before the :// indicates the protocol (in this example, http indicates that

*Figure 3.1* An example of a website address

---

1 E-mail addresses take a similar form with the user name appearing before the @ with the host computer (where the mailbox resides) appearing after the @ and before the domain name (indicating the type of institution housing the mailbox) (e.g. d.d.dolowitz@bham.ac.uk is the mailbox for d.d dolowitz residing at the University of Birmingham, UK)

the document is being accessed through the *Hypertext Transfer Protocol*). The protocol provides your computer with the information it needs to achieve compatibility with the resource you are trying to access. The protocol governing most web-based documents is the Hypertext Transfer Protocol (http). While http:// is the most common protocol you will access online, some of the other protocols you may come across are: ftp://, gopher://, and telnet://. Note that the symbol :// after the protocol is there to separate the protocol from the rest of the address and serves no further function – but is a necessary component of Internet addresses.

Immediately following the protocol is the domain name (www.liv.ac.uk). For you, this is the most important section of the address and it breaks down into three parts.[2] Looking to Figure 3.1 from right to left, the first component – **uk** – indicates the country where the server is located (United Kingdom), the second – **liv.ac** – indicates the name and type of organisation housing the server, and finally, the **www**, indicates the actual server housing the information. While most websites operate www addresses, you will encounter other servers. For example, many European Union sites operate on the 'europa' server. As such, they would be accessed by entering http://europa.eu.int, with the **eu** indicating the organisation (European Union) and the **int** indicating that it is an international organisation.

Probably the two most vital pieces of information you will need for guessing the actual address of an organisation's home page are the organisational code and the country code. The first generally falls into one of six categories.

- **.co** (or **.com**) Commercial organisation (e.g. http://www.dante.com refers to the fictitious company Dante).
- **.ac** or **.edu** Educational institution (e.g. http://www.liv.ac.uk refers to the homepage of the University of Liverpool). In the USA educational establishments are identified by **.edu** (e.g. http://www.utah.edu).

---

2 The domain name can appear as numbers. This provides the same information as discussed but takes the form of the computer housing the information's IP address.

- **.mil** Military site (e.g. http://www.army.mil refers to the homepage of the US Army).
- **.gov** Government department or agency or institution (e.g. http://www.fco.gov.uk refers to the home page of the UK Foreign and Commonwealth Office).
- **.org** Non-commercial organisation not included in any of the other categories (e.g. the United Nations homepage is located at http://www.un.org). Some organisations will be indicated by **.int** – international.
- **.net** Internet resource or service provider.

For all non-US sites, the second element consists of the unique two-letter country code. Every country has its own two-letter code: some of the most common that you might encounter, for example, are:

| | | | |
|---|---|---|---|
| **.uk** | United Kingdom | **.it** | Italy |
| **.de** | Germany | **.ru** | Russia |
| **.au** | Australia | **.fr** | France |

Knowing the protocol and the site's domain name should be enough to help you go to the homepage of almost any organisation you may want to find. Of course, the address of a more specific file that you might want will contain further elaborations which specify the actual path or folder construction leading to the final part of the address, the name of file you are looking at (each folder is separated by a forward slash – / – until the final file). While the path for some files is quite complicated, once you realise that all that the path indicates is the folder/s leading to a file, it is sometimes possible to figure out how to go directly to many detailed sites.[3] In our earlier example the *dolowitz/poli229* is telling the computer to open the folder *dolowitz*, then look in the file called *poli229*.

A key point to remember is that if you do not enter a specific file name after the initial protocol and domain name, the com-

---

3 While most addresses end in a forward slash (/) it is not necessary to include this when entering an address into a browser. However, it may help reduce the time required to download the site if you do.

puter will look for an index page for the folder you end the address with (if there is none it will work back through the previous folders). It also worth remembering that if you are successful in finding a particular file, you might then want to continue truncating the address to the next folder to access a broader index, which will generally expand your information base. So, in the above example, once you have visited http://www.liv.ac.uk/dolowitz/poli229 and found the information you wanted in the file poli229, you can then truncate the address to http://liv.ac.uk/dolowitz to get more general information. As we shall see in the next chapter, this information becomes important when you are trying to assess the quality and credibility of the information you access.

### General subject directories

No matter how much you know about the structure and content of web addresses there will be times when you need to utilise one or more of the search tools that have been developed to help you find information. Whilst it is tempting to jump straight to your favourite search engine, unless you know specifically what you are looking for, the most useful tool to start off with is probably going to be a subject directory. As their name implies, rather than directing you to a specific site containing a keyword or phrase of the sort you enter into a search engine, subject directories are organised around specific subjects. This allows you to explore a topic in considerable detail. Subject directories are less random than automated search engines, and they are all designed, catalogued and maintained by human beings, often experts in the subject. Most directories have been designed to allow you to begin by accessing a general topic and then follow clearly established and maintained hypertext links to sub-directories containing more specialised information, all the way to individual files containing very detailed information. For example, upon entering most general subject directories you will find a list of ten to fourteen general topic headings, which you can then burrow through. One of the most common categories is social science. From this you can burrow your way to detailed information on US political parties (see Figure 3.2).

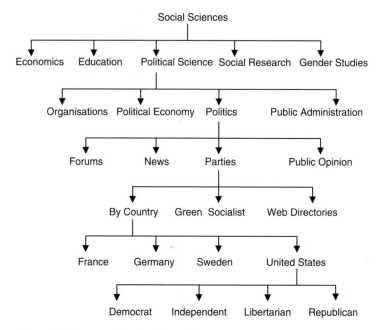

*Figure 3.2* An example of a directories tree

Subject directories themselves come in a variety of forms, some more general in the categories they start from and some more specific. Both sorts are likely to prove useful to you, as are many of the directories dedicated to locating newsgroups and listservers.

General subject directories tend to be provided by large commercial organisations, which are themselves sometimes associated with the page you find yourself starting on after logging on. Probably the largest and best known example of a subject directory, which includes a directory dedicated to the social sciences, is Yahoo! (http://www.yahoo.co.uk or http://www.yahoo.com). As a large directory, not only does Yahoo! include specific resources directing you to general information sources but it also has fourteen general subject directories containing hundreds of subcategories (see Figure 3.3).

Working along similar lines, but containing substantially more information directly relevant to students of politics and

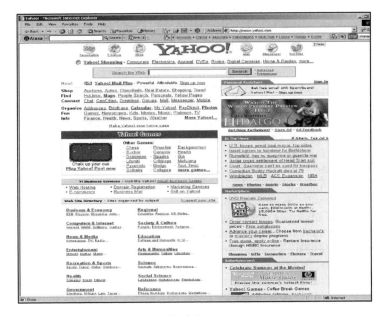

*Figure 3.3*  An example of a subject directory

international relations is LookSmart (http://search.looksmart.
com). LookSmart is an example of a resource that accepts paid
placements, so that some of its sites might be of less use to the
researcher than to advocates or the 'politically motivated'. An
example of a slightly different kind of directory is the Open
Directory Project (http://www.dmoz.org). This is a directory
compiled by 'volunteer' editors who tend to eliminate dead links
much faster than on other directories and which has numerous
directories relating directly to students of politics.

While there are many more general subject directories, because
of their social science related sub-directories, Yahoo!, Look Smart
and the Open Directory Project are three of the better general
directories for politics students. However, there are a number of
directories that have been developed by academics, making them
especially useful for the learning process. One good example of
this kind of directory is the Librarians' Index to the Internet
(http://www.lii.org). This facility is sponsored by California State

Library and uses subject specialists to develop and vet the information contained in its sub-directories. This ensures the quality of the information provided will be capable of fulfilling academic standards. In addition, Infomine (http://infomine.ucr.edu), SOSIG (http://www.sosig.ac.uk) and BUBL (http://bubl.ac.uk) offer general directories dedicated to providing excellent scholarly information. Maintained by the University of California, Riverside, Infomine is a general directory compiled by librarians from a number of US universities, making it one of the best scholarly resources available on the Internet. As an academically established and maintained resource, Infomine links to very specific resources such as online textbooks, databases, journals and special conference proceedings.

While Infomine is a US-based directory, BUBL has established itself as the national information service for Higher Education in the UK. BUBL's subject-specific directories contain sites making it possible to undertake a quick and credible overview of almost any social science discipline or area. However, it should be noted that like all subject directories, BUBL 'neither claims nor aims to be comprehensive as regards resources within any one subject area, but only to provide a quick, user-friendly lead into key resources in any major subject area' (http://bubl.ac.uk/). Finally, the Social Science Information Gateway (SOSIG) is a general subject directory containing over 50,000 social science web pages. And, like the other two, the cataloguers of SOSIG make clear that they see the directory's primary aim as providing 'a trusted source of selected, high quality Internet information in the social sciences' (http://www.sosig.ac.uk/about_us/what_is.html). One feature of SOSIG worth noting is that brief initial descriptions of the resources to be found in its database are also provided, helping to make searches more effective and targeted.

### Clearinghouse subject directories

If you are not familiar with the various directories that are useful for the search that you are engaged in, you can refer to the several clearinghouses dedicated to cataloguing online directories. Good examples of the two main kinds of clearinghouse are the Argus Clearinghouse (http://www.clearinghouse.net) and Searchability (http://www.searchability.com). The Argus Clearinghouse is a directory of over 400 guides compiled by experts, to ensure you are directed to the most relevant general and subject-specific directories and information. It contains directories you can burrow through and provides overviews and keywords for each link, making it possible to judge the site's relevance before burrowing though the link while at the same time helping to provide good tips for further research. Searchibility works in a slightly different way, directing you to specific-subject relevant search tools, regardless of whether they are directories or not. Dedicated to finding specialised subject-based search tools (including those dedicated to searching for information on the 'invisible web'), and providing hints as to how to improve your search techniques, Searchibility is the kind of site that is particularly useful when you first start your research.

### Subject-specific directories

While general subject directories can help direct you to information on almost any subject you can imagine, subject-specific or targeted directories have been developed to jump start your research into very specific fields of study. These include directories dedicated to social science and political topics. It is always a good idea to consider placing sites of this sort that you have found useful into your bookmark/favourites file so that you can easily re-access them in the future.

An example of one of the best subject-specific sites that politics students might access is the University of Keele's Political Science Resource Page (http://www.psr.keele.ac.uk). As the name suggests, this site targets political science resources, allowing you to burrow though specialised information relating to British and international politics. A similar directory, Political Information. Com (http://www.politicalinformation.com) provides a series of sub-directory gateways to range of high-quality information on current political issues. Another targeted directory with politics resources is hosted by the University of British Columbia's Library (http://www.library.ubc.ca/poli/). While this site offers high quality links, it is also worth mentioning because it highlights a very important aspect of subject-specific directories.

Often the best directories are compiled and found at university libraries. As such, it is always worth accessing the library pages of any respected university to see what types of directories have been established by their staff experts before jumping into the wider Internet.

Many of the kind of resources we are looking at here can be accessed through specialised directories and databases found on what we referred to in chapter 2 as the invisible web. In view of this, it is always worth looking for directories dedicated to cataloguing the resources available on the invisible web. A good example is the Invisible Web Directory (http://www.invisible-web.net). This contains numerous sub-directories dedicated to government, social science, news sites, and expert finders that are only available on the invisible web. Another good example is called ProFusion (http://www.profusion.com). One of the key advantages of this site is that it combines subject directories with a search engine, making it possible to refine searches after enough information has been gathered though your initial burrows.

While chapter 2 discussed many of the resources available though subject directories and gateways, one further directory worth mentioning is Top Ten (http://www.toptenlinks.com). This can be classified as a general subject directory, but has an additional feature in that it lists what people actually using the web regard as the best subject directories in the area under review. As such, it can be a very valuable place to begin finding information on subject-specific databases, media sources, government resources, and the different groups that are operating online.

Two additional types of specialist directory that you should be aware of are those dedicated to finding and posting newsgroup listings and those that find and organise listservs into useful categories. As we saw earlier, these are two of the best ways to interact with other individuals and experts interested in the same issues as you are. However, finding those newsgroups and listservs dedicated to your areas of interest may not always be that easy and a directory will be of help. An example of a large directory of newsgroups and newsgroup postings is the Google Group Directory (http://groups-beta.google.com). Google has over a billion postings, searchable by topic and arranged under the following categories:

- **Alt** Contains groups concerned with alternative views, topics and subjects.
- **News** These groups are dedicated to discussing issues surrounding newsgroups.
- **Biz** These groups are dedicated to discussing business-related issues, reviews, services, etc.
- **Rec** Is concerned with groups dedicated to discussing recreational activities.
- **Comp** Is a directory of groups interested in discussing almost every and any computer-related issue.
- **Sci** These groups are dedicated to discussing issues that relate both to the social and the physical sciences.
- **Humanities** This directory is dedicated to groups interested in arts and humanities including issues associated with art, literature, philosophy, history, etc.
- **Soc** Is the directory dedicated to groups concerned with social and cultural topics.
- **Misc** The groups found in this directory are interested in discussing almost any topic not contained in any of the above directories.
- **Talk** The Talk directory contains groups concerned with discussions of current issues and debates. Although, unlike the other newsgroups, this category of sites often abound with unsupported personal opinions, rumours and speculation.

An example of a slightly different kind of directory here is Topica (http://lists.topica.com). Although, like Google, Topica organises its subject directories according to topics, its directories tend to be more intuitively organised for students of social science. This is because three of its major directories are organised so as to cover newsgroups interested in: News and Media, including newsgroups concerned with current and world affairs; Humanities, which includes social science sub-directories; and Government, which houses a number of sub-directories dealing with almost every aspect of politics and government.

Like newsgroups, listservs are also generally best accessed through directories. The directories cataloguing listservs tend to work in one of two ways, sub-dividing them either alphabetically or by type. Either way, however, once you enter the sub-directory you will be provided with the names and descriptions of listservs, and the information you need to join. While there are dozens of listserv directories available, three commonly used examples are ListUniverse.Com (http://tile.net/lists), Cata-List (http://www. lsoft.com/lists/listref.html), and the Mailing List Gurus Page (http://lists.gurus.com). This last site is worth mentioning because it relates to another way of finding information on the web, 'guru pages'. These are websites developed by individual experts and enthusiasts on a given topic which act as mini subject directory or gateway to what they judge to be the best available information on the web.

### *Search engines*

While subject directories are the best place to explore a topic, once you have an understanding of your subject, you are more likely have the confidence to go directly to a specific site where you know the information needed is likely to be found, or to sift through a number of search results for quality and relevance. In this context, search engines are usually your best tool. Unlike directories, which, as we noted earlier, are compiled by human beings who generally have specialist expertise and allow you to burrow your way through a topic, search engines are vast databases containing websites that have been collected by computer programs (spiders and crawlers) that are unique to that particular search engine. As such, one of the key differences between engines and directories is that while you burrow your way though a directory, when you enter a search term into an engine it can return anything from a few to many thousands of hits depending on how it indexes its database and on the particular search terms you have entered.

Despite the vast number of returns you may often receive, when you use a search engine you are searching not the web itself but the database compiled from the data collected by spiders and crawlers. Because of this, even the engines with the largest databases (such as Google and Alta Vista) only contain about 20 per cent of the possible number of sites that exist on the web at any one time (for more information see: Schlein 2002: 79–87; http://www.infotoday.com/searcher/may01/liddy.htm; http://www.

marketing-internet.nu/seo-articles/how-search-engines-work.htm).

Because each database is unique to its particular search engine, it is always a good idea to conduct your search on more than one engine, no matter how comfortable you are with a particular engine and how large that engine's database. This is because a particular engine might return hits in such a way that the most appropriate to your needs appear after the first thousand useless hits. Engines rank and display returns according to their own unique formulae, so even if two engines return similar sites, they could appear in the return pages in widely differing locations. Another reason for utilising more than one engine is that while all engines have similar basic search features and operating procedures, each has a unique collection of advanced search features. These features allow you to narrow your search parameters so as to maximise the number of relevant returns (for more information on search engines see: Basch and Bates 2000: 43–70; Schlein 2002: 81–6; Websearch, http://www.websearch.about.com; Research-Buzz, http://www.researchbuzz.com; Search Engine Watch, http://www.searchenginewatch.com; Search Engine Showdown, http://www.searchengineshowdown.com).

While the best place to learn about a search engine is its help or FAQ pages, it is always worth having some initial practice at using its basic search features. Using an engine's basic facilities will provide you with practical information on the types of returns and rankings you can expect from different engines and help you decide which engines provide the most relevant returns for your search needs. Once you have some familiarity with the basic features, it is then worth exploring the advanced features of an engine. These features generally allow you to narrow the number and type of returns you receive to the most relevant. Table 3.1 should help you in this process, as it lists a selection of the major all-purpose (general) search engines and the key search features they provide. Looking across the table, it should be apparent that search engines offer numerous ways to limit the number of returns you receive, however the best techniques available on most search engines are: phrase searching, Boolean searches, field searching, and using any limitation functions available.

Clearly the best initial strategy for limiting the relevance and

Table 3.1 Search engines

| Search engines | Boolean | Default | Proximity | Truncation | Case | Fields | Limits | Stop | Sorting |
|---|---|---|---|---|---|---|---|---|---|
| **Google**<br>http://www.google.com | –, OR | and | Phrase | No | No | in title, in url, more | Language, file type, date, more | Yes, + searches | Relevance, site |
| **AlltheWeb**<br>http://www.alltheweb.com | AND, OR, AND NOT, (), +, –, OR WITH () | and | Phrase | No | No | title, URL, link, more | Language, file type, date, more | No | Relevance, site |
| **HotBot (Inktomi)**<br>http://www.hotbot.com | AND, OR, NOT, (), – | and | Phrase | No | Yes | title, more | Language, date, more | Some | Relevance, site |
| **MSN Search**<br>http://search.msn.com | AND, OR, NOT, (), – | and | Phrase | No | Yes | title, link | Language, filetype, date, more | Some | Relevance |
| **Teoma**<br>http://teoma.com | –, OR | and | Phrase | No | No | intitle, inurl | Language, site | Yes, + searches | Relevance, metasites |
| **Gigablast**<br>http://gigablast.com | AND, OR, NOT, (), +, – | or | Phrase, NEAR | No | No | Title, site, ip, more | No | No | Relevance, date |

| *Meta-search engines* | Search Engines capable of searching more than one database at a time but are restricted to the lowest common denominator search parameters. |
| --- | --- |
| **Excite Meta-Search**<br>http://www.excite.com | Searches a number of partner databases and has the ability to display up to thirty returns per page and collect thirty results from each database |
| **Dogpile**<br>http://www.dogpile.com | Allows you to choose up to eighteen different search tools and is capable of employing Boolean operators. |
| **Ask Jeeves**<br>http://www.askjeeves.com | Allows you to search with questions rather than precise terms or phrases. However, it is best to keep the questions simple. Returns the best search engines for conducting your search rather than specific sites |
| **MetaCrawler**<br>http://www.metacrawler.com | Searches a number of databases, has the ability to display up to thirty returns and collect thirty returns from each database. It also eliminates duplicate results and has easy to follow and use return pages. |
| **Savvy Search**<br>http://www.savvysearch.com | Searches 1,000 databases, categorises them based on the type of resource they were drawn from and allows you to sort the results by date, source and relevance. |

Adapted from Search Engine Showdown (http://www.searchengineshowdown.com), by Greg R. Notess number of returns is to use terms that are as specific or distinctive as possible; it can also be a useful technique to enter a longer phrase when initiating searching. The key feature of search engines is that they will produce results which reflect exactly what you have typed into them, which is clearly a very powerful limiting mechanism. Often, the best way to start is by entering keywords, although remember that when you do this, most engines will look for documents in which each word you have entered figures, no matter how far apart the words appear in the document (unless you can provide the engine with a proximity figure – a feature of Alta Vista) and regardless of whether they are related to one another in any particular fashion. However, there are two basic ways to tell an engine to return only sites containing your exact phrase. First, you can use " ", which tells the engine to find exactly what is contained in the quotation marks. Second, if you access the advanced search features section of most engines, you will be provided with a range of limiting options including one requiring the engine to return hits including only the exact phrases you enter.

In addition to phrase searching the next strategy for limiting the number of returns in terms both of relevance and numbers is to use your engine's 'Boolean' functions. While this might sound complicated, all it refers to are the AND (+), OR and NOT (–) commands. The AND functions much as phrase searching in that putting AND between search terms tells the engine that both terms must be included in any hit. However, it is also useful because it can be used to connect two or more phrases as well as terms. Thus you might be interested in finding sites discussing both the UK Labour Party and the American Democratic Party. In this instance, two possible ways to begin limiting the number of returns would be to use phrase searching or to use the Boolean AND function:

- 'Democrats' + 'Labour'

or

- 'US Democratic Party' AND 'UK Labour Party'

Similarly, the NOT function allows you to tell the engine that you want one term or phrase but not another. This can be very useful for eliminating returns where the term or phrase you are looking for is associated with a number of different sub-terms or phrases. For example, if you are looking for information on Bill Clinton but want to know about his policies rather than about the vagaries of his private life, you could limit the returns by entering

- 'Clinton' NOT 'Affair'

or

- 'Bill Clinton' – 'Monica Lewinski'

Finally, if you want to maximise the amount of information you receive on related topics you might use OR. This will tell the engine to return information on either or both of the terms and/or phrases you enter. So, if you are interested in documents containing information on the American presidency and the Democratic Party you might enter

- 'American presidency' OR 'Democratic Party'

Entering this will return tell the search engine to return sites containing America, the Democratic Party and those containing both American and the Democratic Party.

When you are engaging in searches, it is always worth keeping in mind is that you can mix and match Boolean operators to create a very limited search. This noted, there is a further technique you can use, known as 'field searching', which allows you to limit your search to a specific part of an Internet document. In many cases, all you have to do is access the advanced search features of the engine and tick the appropriate box or menu item. Alternatively, you can engage in a field search by starting your search phrase with the field followed immediately by a colon (:), and then the search term or phrase. While each engine will have more or fewer fields available, some of the most useful fields are: TITLE, which limits returns to documents whose title includes the search term; URL, which limits the returns to only those where the address contains your search term; DOMAIN, which limits your search to only those documents whose domain name ends with your search term/s; and finally, LINK, which will return documents which are hypertext linked to sites containing your search terms.

One further useful way of limiting your search is by reference to the category of document to be found. Again, this is generally done through the advanced search features of the engine and allows you to limit your searches to particular dates, languages, file-type (e.g. ftp, html, Mp3), and domain. For example, Google allows you to limit your search by date and also by language. Thus, if you are interested in the most recent information relating to German opinion towards the Euro, once you have entered appropriate search terms, you can then limit your search to documents placed into Google's database within the past three months, and only those pages written in German.

### *Specialised search engines*

While general and meta-search engines contain the largest databases, provide the most versatility and return the largest number of hits, at times you will want an engine that focuses on a specific topic or type of search. It is important, therefore, to acquaint yourself with some of the specialised search engines that are available to help you search the Internet.

### *People finders*

Among the most useful search engines in the research process are those designed to help you find and contact other individuals. Foremost amongst these are the various search engines dedicated to finding telephone numbers and addresses. While it is often possible to find a person through a general search engine, there are some very good people-finding engines capable of assisting your search. For example, if all you are interested in is finding a phone number or addresses of a person you want to talk to, there are a number of search engines dedicated to nothing but compiling lists of phone numbers and addresses. While no one online phonebook will access anything like all the numbers and addresses that exist today, three good examples of online phonebooks are the People-Search (http://www.peoplesearch.net); Teldir (http://www.infobel.com/teldir/); and Global Yellow Pages (http://www.globalyp.com/world.htm). The added advantage of these particular search engines is that each incorporates a multi-country look-up capability and meta-search engine capabilities, allowing them to utilise a range of specialised phonebooks in their search. They also have reverse look-up capabilities. Reverse look-up allows you to enter a phone number or address and discover to whom it belongs. This is clearly useful if, as sometimes happens, you record a number or address but then forget whose it is.

In addition to phonebooks there are a number of search engines dedicated to looking up e-mail addresses. While e-mail information tends to go out of date rather quickly, as experts move from one institution to another or change providers, e-mail finders can be useful starting points when trying to locate a particular individual or expert. A number of available e-mail finders only search US addresses, but two that operate internationally are: ICQ (http://www.icq.com/whitepages) and WED (http://www.worldemail.com). As with telephone and address finders, these tools tend to have reverse look-up capabilities.

## *Expert finders*

One of the best ways of finding experts in any given area of study is to go to the sites belonging to universities and research institutions and then go to the home pages of the department or school dealing with that subject area and look to see who is working on it, what they say about it, and how you can contact them. While this is one of the most direct means of finding and contacting experts, another technique is to use specialised search engines or expert finders, which may help broaden the range of your search. There are many expert finders available, but some good examples are Facsnet (http://facsnet.org), which has wide coverage and provides information on experts working not only in academia but also in think tanks, government agencies, and the private sector. Another good example is IRE (http://www.ire.org/resourcecenter/initial-search-beat.html). This is primarily targeted at journalists looking for specific information but nevertheless has a broad range and is of particular interest as it has a good collection of experts on social and political issues. Ask an Expert (http://www.askanexpert.com) is useful because it provides the e-mail addresses of experts who have volunteered to answer your questions, greatly increasing the likelihood that your query will meet with a positive response. Reference Desk (http://www.refdesk.com/expert.html) is a final specialised search engine worth mentioning because it is an engine dedicated to locating other expert finders, allowing you to maximise your search potential.

### Automating searches with software tools

One of the most useful recent developments for students, academics and researchers interested in utilising the web has been the creation of software programs that are downloaded onto your hard drive and installed (as a tool bar) inside your web browser, which track the sites you access and then offer you a list of related sites based on the aggregated browsing habits of everyone utilising the software. Three examples of such packages that you can use with Netscape and/or Internet Explorer are Copernic (http://www.copernic.com), Alexa (http://www.alexa.com), and Ucmore (http://www.ucmore.com). By offering you a list of related sites, these programs not only expand your research potential but they help to concentrate your searches to the most relevant sites. In addition, most of these programs can help you begin to evaluate the quality of the websites you visit. This is because most of these software packages allow you to access the preference information relating to the site you are viewing, dramatically enhancing your ability to judge the authority and credibility of the site.

### The professionals

A final set of search tools you might consider using are the professional online services. While these services charge a fee they can often prove very useful. As with the tools discussed so far, there are hundreds of fee-based or professional online services available to help you conduct your research. Sometimes these services can provide you with information you can get from no other source on the Internet, including public records, legal decisions, conference papers, scholarly journal articles and papers, and many other kinds of documents. These services have been developed to scour thousands of data sources, so that a single search can turn up either vast amounts of information or a particular record or document, all depending on what you are looking for. Moreover, as these are professional services that depend on paying customers for their survival, they are usually very concerned to ensure the reliability and quality of the information they produce, which is not always true of online information sources. Of these services the one most commonly subscribed to by universities is LexisNexis (http://www.lexisnexis.com). LexisNexis offers four different professional search engines covering law, business, government and the academic world. Whichever service you use, LexisNexis offers one of the largest collections of academically relevant information available online. A similar service, drawing on the full-text versions of the information contained in over 7,500 publications, documents and records is the Dialog (http://www.dialogweb.com) research service. Another, slightly different professional service, is Northern Light (http://www.northernlight.com). While Northern Light started life as a free service, it has become one of the main academic fee-based sites available. It differs from many other professional services in that it allows you to search its databases and pay for individual items without having to pay a monthly or yearly membership fee. This feature makes Northern Light useful for those who only need to resort to professional services for occasional searches. A further feature of many of these professional services is that they offer an alert facility. This allows you to tell the service to send you e-mail notices whenever its researchers or web crawlers find new information relevant to your area of interest, helping you to keep up to date with the most recent data available.

## Conclusion

A key skill when exploring the web is knowing which tool to use, when to use it, and when it is necessary to use more than one tool to conduct the same search. You will become more skilled in this the more you explore the tools available. However, as a general rule, of the tools that have been developed to help you find your way through the jungle of sites that is the web, subject directories offer the best starting point. These have been designed specifically to offer you a good entry point into a given topic, going from the most general to the specific by drilling through a single database. The key is to use these when you don't have a clear picture of what precisely you are looking for or where you do not have much information but are interested in a topic you know is covered by a subject directory or sub-directory. On the other hand, where you have a good feel of a subject, or have a very specific query, keyword search engines will probably offer the best starting point, returning the widest possibilities of returns but with the ability to restrict these through advanced search techniques. As such, with a little time and effort, no matter how obscure or specific your particular area of interest, it is likely that if there is information relating to it available online and you should be able to find it using one of the search tools discussed in this chapter.

# 4   Evaluating sources

No matter where you are in your learning process you are going to have to develop the capacity to evaluate the quality of the information you encounter. Of course, this is true whether the sources you are using are in books, articles, newspapers or on the Internet. However, judging the quality of sources has been made easier in most traditional paper-based sources of data, not only because they tend to provide you with easily identifiable clues by which to judge their accuracy and quality but also because many of these sources have already gone though extensive processes of peer review and academic assessment, particularly articles appearing in scholarly journals and books published by the major publishing houses. Further, items you find in the university library have gone through a series of steps to ensure their credibility, accuracy and quality, since the majority have either been recommended by an academic or judged to be an important contribution to the library's collection by a subject-specialist librarian. As such, you have a fairly good idea that the data presented in these sources is useable in your research and learning. When it comes to the Internet, on the other hand, these safeguards are often absent and for the most part, anyone can publish anything online. In the light of this it is not surprising that whilst there are undoubtedly some excellent resources available on the Internet, there are equally many sites being put up every day that are biased, opinionated, inaccurate or dubious. Because of this, it is extremely important to make sure that the information you access and utilise is both appropriate for your research and maintains the level of accuracy, credibility and objectivity that is required in an academic context.

The primary focus of this chapter will be on some of the key tools that you can use to evaluate the overall quality of the resources you have been shown how to categorise and find in the previous two chapters.

## Using your existing knowledge

Before going on to discuss some of the more advanced techniques available for evaluating online information some basic considerations are worth noting with which you may already have become familiar if you have experience in using the Internet in your studies. It is clear that some sources of online information are going to be more reliable than others. For example, any online information that has been recommended by your supervisor or module coordinator is likely to be of academic quality. Similarly, if you are directed by an academic or academically related source to an online database, subject directory or other form of portal or site it is more likely to be of academic quality than sources you simply come across whilst browsing the Internet. Further, it is generally safe to assume that sites that have been compiled by an expert or series of subject-specific experts such as SOSIG (http://www.sosig.ac.uk) and Infomine (http://infomine.ucr.edu), which you access while burrowing your way through a subject directory, will probably contain information of appropriate quality. Finally, where such 'reputable' sites provide links to other online resources, these resources can probably be regarded as 'safe', though since these sites are 'foreign' to the original site it becomes more important that you begin to consider some of the techniques and ideas discussed below, especially if you follow other links which take you further and further away from the 'reputable' site from which you started. In general, in order to ensure that you are not being misled by seemingly objective literature, it is wise as a matter of course to evaluate what you read, particularly if you find it online.

## Types of websites

Online resources are particularly difficult to evaluate because anyone can create their own website and then put forward a view regardless of who they are, what authority they have in relation to that topic, how objective they may be, or even what purpose they have in establishing the site. The Internet has proved to be a very popular medium for those who wish to make assertions, publicise personal opinions or engage in public invective. This is mainly because it is relatively inexpensive in comparison to more traditional forms of publication and because it is relatively easy to learn how to write directly onto the web or transfer information produced using other software programs directly onto a personal or organisational site. Moreover, as we noted earlier, unlike more traditional sources of information, most of the material available on the Internet has not been subjected to any form of professional scrutiny, making it much more difficult to judge its objectivity or accuracy.

It is therefore important that you use a variety of techniques to judge not only the usefulness of online information for your learning purposes but also the quality of that information. Of course, how far you go with this will depend on the particular purpose you have in seeking information online. For example, if you only want to use online information to help support an oral argument with a friend, you might not need to spend a great deal of time trying to judge either the accuracy or objectivity of the information. However, if you want to use the same information to support an argument presented in a final year dissertation project, knowing something about how to evaluate the information presented on the site should give you some clues as to how much credence you should give it.

One of the initial ways in which you might begin to scrutinise the information you have discovered is to consider exactly what type of document you are dealing with. Different documents may need to be looked at in different ways and some will require greater care than others. You might ask yourself some basic questions: Is the document a news story produced by a major online newspaper or magazine? Is it an academic article contained in a major refereed journal? Is it a document written by a particular political party to persuade you of the correctness of their particular policy or programme? Is it a piece of information placed on the net by an ideologically driven partisan? Knowing what type of site you have accessed will help you to begin to make these judgments and help to begin assessing the objectivity of the information you find. Almost any document placed online can be categorised according to who posted it online and what purpose they had in doing so. To help you begin to recognise the differences here, we will present a general schema adapted from the work of Ó Dochartaigh (2002), which places web documents on a continuum running from advocacy documents that can contain considerable bias and 'inaccuracies' all the way to well-researched, authoritative documents produced by reputable government organisations and institutions.

### *Advocacy documents*

Some of the hardest documents to assess are those produced by individuals and groups advocating a particular perspective, argument or goal. Examples of groups who may produce such material include political parties and the many kinds of pressure groups that operate online. Similarly, individuals who have a particularly strong view on an issue or topic may produce an advocacy document or participate in a newsgroup or listserv discussion. Once you recognise that you are actually reading an advocacy document it is important to remember that the quality and nature of these documents varies, with some being produced deliberately to distort information so as to support the point of view of that group or individual, while others are well researched and are used to present as fair and rigorous an argument as possible. Therefore, you must be careful to evaluate and use advocacy documents appropriately.

Equally, once you realise that you have found an advocacy document you must consider its appropriateness as a source of information for your research. While it is clear that many advocacy documents are good for helping you learn about opposing or untraditional views, there is little doubt that the information on these sites should be viewed with caution, as it may be distorted to benefit the individual's or organisation's argument. Because of this, if you do decide to use an advocacy document in your research ensure you evaluate it very carefully, place what it says in the context of the particular standpoint it may be expressing, and always try to consult and where necessary include documents that present opposing viewpoints.

### *Personal web pages*

A different, although often closely associated, type of source is the personal web page – documents placed on the web by an individual wishing to make personal information available to anyone with access to the Internet. Often you may feel it is appropriate to use the information contained on such sites, particularly as sometimes they may be the only place where such information is available, since the Internet might be the only place the individual could get their views published and considered. Again, however, these sites need to be treated with care. As with any advocacy document you find on the Internet, when working with documents of this sort, think about what the individual is saying and what qualifications they have to be talking about the subject. You need not simply dismiss all individual web pages just because they only contain one person's viewpoint, for often these people are recognised experts who have utilised personal web pages to present new information, to summarise arguments made elsewhere, or to enhance the work of advocacy groups that they support. However, it is wise when using these sites to consider who the author is and what their credentials might be; and as with advocacy sites, it is always worth referring to other sources on the same topic that might present a different picture of the issues or presentation of the facts.

### *News and corporate documents*

There are a vast number of news and corporate sources on the web, representing a variety of views from across the world. While little of this information will go through the same level of peer and/or academic review as it would in online academic documents, in general, corporate and news documents provide you with good quality, credible information, particularly those produced by well-known, reputable sources such as the BBC (http://www.bbc.co.uk), the New York Times (http://www.nytimes.com), or Microsoft (http://www.microsoft.com). Not only can these sources help provide you with an idea of what is being discussed in the public domain but the Internet also makes it easier to search archives produced by these sources quickly and easily.

However, when you use information produced by corporations or online news sources, remember that, while you can generally be more certain of the quality of the information than you can with advocacy or personal web pages, the information may be biased in some way. For instance, newspaper journalists can be writing from a viewpoint that expresses a particular political line or perspective. Additionally, as many media sources depend upon advertising revenue, it is possible that the information presented is adapted so as to ensure, for example, that their advertisers do not take any offence. Equally, in journalistic contexts, stories that are perceived to have a high news value will often have more importance attached to them; and this not necessarily based on the wider importance or significance of the topic. For example, international news coverage is often limited in British papers, as these kinds of stories are not perceived to be of great interest to the British public. Thus, it is important that you do some research to determine as much as you can about the news source in order to use the information contained in it appropriately. Think, for example, about the political leanings of the paper, about who owns it and about the readership at which it is aimed. Similarly, always remember that regardless of the quality of the information you find on a corporate site, the aim of these sites is to promote and sell the company and that they may only be giving you one viewpoint. Again, as with advocacy pages, it is always a good idea when using these sites to try and find other sources that will help you check the information and/or provide an alternative perspective.

### Academic documents

Generally, the most reliable and objective sources of online information are the documents produced by academics or those sites which contain useful academic resources. In the main, these are likely to be articles on a site that is an online version of a well-known paper-based journal or articles in one of a number of new electronic journals. In addition, you may find documents produced by academics testing out new ideas or presenting the early results of research that is still progress. In this category you may, for example, find articles in published conference proceedings, papers presented at workshops and other 'official' gatherings, and sometimes documents that have been specifically written for and produced on corporate websites.

Work by academics can be very useful as in the majority of cases these documents are likely to be closest in level and style to the kind of work that you are expected to do at university. However, always evaluate and use the information appropriately, considering the kind of academic article it is and what your purpose is in using it. Similarly, remember that just because it was written by an academic and published after a peer-review process does not mean that you have to take all that it says as 'given'. You can still critically evaluate it in terms of the quality of the research, the strength of the argument and how it fits in with the rest of your knowledge on a particular topic.

### *Official documents*

A further category of sources is that consisting of official documents, produced by any public institution or agency ranging from individual governmental agencies and institutions all the way to the major international organisations such as NATO (http:// www.nato.int) and the UN (http://www.un.int). You can usually assume that if a document is part of a government website then it is an official document and that the information contained will be authoritative, accurate and fairly objective. As with academic sources, you may generally find the information in official documents reasonably straightforward to use in your work and less in need of critical scrutiny than that provided in the other categories we have discussed. However, still read official documents with a view to identifying a particular viewpoint and always balance this with counter-arguments. It is also worth noting that some public institutions will have a publicity department or section that releases information to the press and other broadcast media. When you find documents produced by this section of an institution it may be advisable, whilst remaining aware of their origin, to treat these more like news sources rather than strictly as official documents. There may well be en element of 'spin' that you will need to look out for.

## Internet address evaluation

Having identified various types of document and thought about the level of scrutiny they might need, we can now consider how best to identify and categorise a particular document. In many cases, it might be quite obvious to which of the above categories a document belongs but this is not always the case. Where it is not, a careful look at the site address can be helpful. As discussed in chapter 3, the individual URL addresses that each Internet site is provided with contains a considerable amount of information that you can use to determine the type of site and document you have accessed. For instance, as a general rule personal web pages will contain a person's name proceeded by a tilde (~) or a percent sign (%). When you see this information in the URL address you know that even if the page is linked to an official site it is highly likely that the company or institution hosting the page is not monitoring it, even if the site is contained on the server of a university of other academic institutions. Similarly, because it is fairly easy for anyone to purchase a domain name and then place their own sites on it, you are likely sometimes to see sites which have an official look about them but are actually personal or advocacy pages. You therefore generally need to be quite careful how you assess and use the information placed on a site containing either tildes or percent signs, as this information has probably not been checked in terms of its objectivity or in terms of the author's credentials.

When assessing a website address, the domain name also potentially provides a wealth of information about the organisation on whose server the information has been placed. As you may recall from chapter 3, if, for example, you see **.edu** or **.ac** in the domain, this generally indicates that you are visiting the site of an academic institution; **.gov** indicates you have accessed a government website; **.int** generally indicates you have accessed an international organisation; **.org** tends to indicate you have found a non-profit or advocacy site; while **.com** or **.co** generally indicates that you are looking at documentation produced by a corporation. It is always useful to notice these details: without looking at the higher level domain, for example, it is fairly easy to classify an advocacy site as an academic site. This is a common mistake as some advocacy sites call themselves by titles that include formal-sounding terms such as 'Institute' (such as the Adam Smith Institute, http:// www.adamsmith.org, or the Cato Institute, http://www.cato.org); 'Centre' (Center for Defense Information, http://www.cdi.org, or Centre for Independent Studies, http://www.cis.org.au); and 'Foundation' (such as the Foundation for Economic Education, http://www.fee.org). All of these sites are in fact advocacy sites dedicated to the spread of a particular ideological view concerning public, social and economic policy. Another feature of addresses to look out for is the country code. When a document contains the code of a country whose institutions you are not familiar with, it is important to discover who published it, for this is occasionally another way of hiding highly opinionated pieces behind a veneer of respectability. In general, then, you should always begin your analysis of a website by looking at the URL.

## Site evaluation

Having looked at some types of sites you are likely to come across, and at some of the pitfalls they may contain, it is worth looking in a little more detail at the evaluation techniques that have been developed to help you determine the value and quality of the information you access online. These are techniques that you are expected to employ when you use online research as part of your work. In general, the emphasis here is on the importance of determining the accuracy, authority, objectivity, currency and coverage of the information. First, it is important to stress once again that the way you evaluate different documents will depend on their source and what you want to do with the information. Thus, the ways in which you analyse and use an advocacy paper will be different from those you employ with an official document. For example, an advocacy website will not be objective in the same sense as you would expect an academic researcher's website to be. However, this does not necessarily mean you should dismiss the advocacy site, as its purpose is different. It can help to provide you with a different type of data that might be of use in some contexts but not others. With this in mind, the remainder of this section will be dedicated to a brief discussion of the key areas you should consider when evaluating Internet sites.

## Scope and audience

Before spending a great deal of time analysing the accuracy, authority or objectivity of a document, you should spend a moment thinking about both its scope and its intended audience, for these set the stage for any further analysis. So, you can ask yourself if the document is intended to provide an overview of a topic or is designed to focus on a very specific element of a much larger argument or issue. You can also ask yourself whether the document fulfils your individual expectations of what it should cover. If it does not, you might ask yourself if you should bother using the site as a source of information.

Similarly, it is worth considering whom the site is targeting for its audience. If the site presents very technical information and all you are looking for is background information, the site might not have been developed for your learning needs. Similarly, if you visit an advocacy site but are looking for a neutral source of information, clearly you have visited the wrong site for the information you require.

## Accuracy and credibility

Once you have determined that you are interested in a site and that it is appropriate for your needs, you will need to consider how accurate the information presented on the site is. Any good site should present data in a way such that you can verify what is offered as fact. When attempting to verify the accuracy of any data presented on a website, one of the first questions you should ask goes back to the purpose or intent of the site. Remember that some sites are not intended to present an accurate view and, as such, you should not expect the data on these sites to be truthful. If you determine that the site has been established to present an accurate representation of the data being discussed, one way you can begin to verify the information is to simply examine the overall appearance of the site. For example, how much faith do you want to place in a site that contains grammar and spelling errors or where there are a number of typographical mistakes? How much faith do you want to place in a site if little or none of the information can be verified? Similarly, how much credibility should be given to a site that only refers you to other online sites that cannot be verified themselves?

In this process it is worth remembering that you can always rely on your existing knowledge. In other words, if the information you find does not make sense, given your existing knowledge base, or runs counter to what you have already discovered, this should be a warning, telling you to begin questioning the reliability of what you have found. However, you do not have to rely solely on your own knowledge. In addition to the hints provided above, you might also want to consider whether the resource is up to date, uses appropriate sources, and has active external links to the information sources used. You might also consider factors such as the design of the page and the care with which the article has been presented and structured. If these basic aspects of the site are not reassuring, then you might want to consider what this tells you about the care with which the authors may have put together their arguments or indeed the importance they attach to the document (Cameron 2001).

Finally, it is often useful to look for any indications that anyone else has evaluated the information before it was placed online. If the document has gone through a peer-review or editorial process (as is generally the case with journal articles published online, newspaper articles and official documents) it is far more likely to contain accurate information than sites that have been placed directly on the web by an individual or advocacy group, with no internal or external check.

### *Authority and credibility*

Not only is it important to make judgments about the accuracy of online information, it is also wise to consider where the information on a site originated, or who provided it (which is, in fact, really part of the same process). Many scholarly sites, as well as most media sites and official publications, make this easy because they clearly label the documents on their sites as belonging to and originating from themselves (telling everyone that they take responsibility for the accuracy of the information contained in the document) and they also tend to include information relating to the author and the institution or company responsible for the document's content. One clear way to determine if a site is authoritative, or that the author had the skills, information and expertise necessary to produce the information presented, is to look for information telling you that the document or data is attributed to a reputable author or organisation, or that enough information is presented for you to research this information.

If there is little information about the author on the site, it becomes all the more important to attempt to find out as much as you can about them. One of the best ways to do this is to conduct a search of the author's name using one of the techniques discussed in chapter 3 or by looking for any other relevant documents that they might have published. It may also, in some cases, be relevant to consider where the document is hosted. A respectable host institution will justify greater confidence in the document. Although remember, again, that belonging to a particular institution does not necessarily imply that an individual's thoughts are automatically more valuable than those of a person who comes from a very different background (Cameron 2001). For example, just because a person is an academic, or you find the document on an academic server, it does not necessarily indicate that the person has the exclusive expertise to make the definitive comment on a particular topic, or that they necessarily have more information than, say, an interest group putting out information on the same topic. Again, checking against other sites or sources will be helpful.

Given the importance of tracing the authority of the source providing the information online, it is worth looking at some of the ways in which you can begin to examine the credibility of the author or site you are considering. Some of the more common techniques include:

- Looking to see if the information being presented is located on the site of a trustworthy organisation, such as a university or government agency.
- Checking that the site and author have been cited by other sources you know to be respectable.
- Looking to see if the information presented is in an area in which the author has published previously.
- Looking for any bibliographical information on the author,

including affiliations or credentials, and seeing if these provide information on their ability to write in this area.

If none of these techniques bring satisfactory results, you might try to contact the author directly if an e-mail or contact address is provided. In cases where you are very interested in the material provided but cannot verify its authority or accuracy, it can be worth contacting a domain registry to find out who paid for the website. This can often tell you a lot about the credibility and authority of the information and of the person responsible for it. While there are many different ways to find out who has registered a particular domain name, a comprehensive list can be found using either http://www.icann.net or http://www.iana.org/cctld/cctld-whois.htm (Schlein 2002).

Whilst it is important to know who has produced the information you are considering using, a further issue that you might want to consider in addition to the direct authorship of a document is how much of the data on the site is first-hand. If the author is presenting data that has passed though a number of 'filters', it is worth considering issues of both accuracy and objectivity and doing some checking. Similarly, if you are using information you find on a mailing list or newsgroup, it is worth considering whether the list is a moderated site, and if so, to what extent the information is being managed or censored. This becomes particularly important in that it raises issues of authenticity. If a site is unmoderated, or if it is impossible to verify the identity of the author, it is worth asking whether the individual or organisation claiming to have produced the information has actually produced it. In general, if the author has withheld their identity it is probably wise to be sceptical about the information presented.

### *Objectivity*

No matter what source you use there may be a slant in the way the information is presented which might influence the way you interpret it. This is true of many sources, from the most reputable publications, such as HM Treasury (http://www.hm-treasury.gov.uk) or the New York Times (http://www.nytimes.com), all the way to highly ideologically driven pressure groups and think tanks such as the Adam Smith Institute (http://www.adamsmith. org) or the Institute of Economic Affairs (http://www.iea.org.uk). As such, it becomes very important to utilise as much information as you can to determine how objective a document is. For most of your academic work you are going to want to find sites which try to minimise bias, for example, by putting forward alternative viewpoints or attempting to overcome potential bias through the selection of participants and the adoption of suitable methods of presentation and analysis.

One question that it is always wise to ask yourself is whether you think that the site or author might have any motives for emphasising one conclusion or point of view over another. You will find some indications that might help you determine this if you always look to see whether the research is sponsored by a commercial organisation, whether there is advertising on the site, or whether the site is part of a commercial or ideologically driven organisation that might have a stake in what is presented. For example, you should not expect the information being presented by a major oil company to present the case for the elimination of the internal combustion engine. Similarly, you should be on the lookout for sites that are little more than cleverly disguised advertisements for a particular product or idea. In other words, if you go to a site dedicated to the spreading of global free trade (e.g. World Bank, http://www.worldbank.org; IMF, http:// www.imf.org), you should not be surprised to find information supporting the role of free trade in the developing world. The same holds true for politics. If you begin to read a negative description of a candidate or political position you might want to be sure you are not on the website of an opposition party or pressure group; you should not expect either of these sources to present an objective picture. All this indicates that when judging a site for its objectivity, you must not only look for bias within the information but also for possible reasons why the information was produced and then placed online above and beyond the desire to disseminate accurate knowledge.

Finally, when considering the objectivity of a website, you should never underestimate how hard it can be to detect even extremist points of view. Many sites have been designed to hide their 'true intent': designers of sites which promote biased and extremist points of view often work very hard at making them look and sound as if they are educational or scholarly assessments of the information. If you have scrutinised a site and are still unsure as to whether it is appropriate to use in your work, it is a good idea to consult your supervisor or module teacher for advice.

Of course, sometimes, documents presenting a particular ideological point of view, or even a particular commercial interest, will be just what you want. Where, for example, you are charting and assessing the ideas of a particular ideological grouping or political party, you will want to seek out sites of this sort as your source material. The important thing, again, is to be aware and discriminating enough to know the kind of material you are dealing with and when and where that material is suitable for use in your work.

### *Currency*

As is the case with other more traditional resources, you should consider how current the information is that you have found. In some areas of research it is vital that you use material that is as current as possible; for other types of research, older sources will be just as appropriate, or sometimes more appropriate. Once you have determined how current your information needs to be, there are a number of ways to begin exploring how suitable the information that you have accessed is for your research. Clearly, if you access online media sources the chances are that the information (unless you enter their archives) will be current, often up to the minute. Similarly, there are a growing number of online journals that will have the latest editions available (though this does not indicate that the article documents current events or uses relevant data sources). This noted, one of the best ways to determine the currency of information on a website is to look for indications as to when the information was first put on the Internet or any reference to the date on which the information was most recently revised. Equally, some of the better sites will also include information on when any of the data utilised by the documentation on the site was collected or analysed. For example, if you access information from the US Census Bureau (http://www.census.gov) it provides the dates on which the information underpinning its statistics was gathered and when the analysis was undertaken.

When no information can be found on a site, it is often possible to truncate the address to the homepage folder. This should have information on when a site was placed on the web or last modified. If this does not work, both Internet Explorer and Netscape Navigator allow you to access the properties of websites. Although many sites do not keep this information up to date, or make it available to the browser, this is another way of determining the currency of the information you are looking at. Another possible indication of how up to date a site is relates to the number of external links that no longer work. If many of the sites to which the document is linked have disappeared (or moved) this may give you an indication that the resource has not been updated recently. If all else fails you can always attempt to contact the author to obtain this information or use a piece of software (http://www. bookmarklets.com) to find more information on the publication date.

### Coverage

A final issue that you should consider when evaluating a website is the overall level of coverage that a site provides in relation to a particular topic. When you read any document you can begin by using your pre-existing knowledge on the subject to consider what (if any) areas are covered by the document that you have not seen elsewhere (i.e. the document's uniqueness) and to consider the value of what is written to your research. For example, you might think about whether there are any areas you would expect the source to highlight that it did not. If the coverage is sketchy you should be wary of the quality of the information contained in the site. Equally, it is always worth reflecting on who the site is aimed at: think about the level at which the information is pitched and look for indications as to whom the author is addressing and whether, in view of this, the source is appropriate for the kind of research you are doing.

## Citing information sources on the web

Once you have become familiar with the primary types of resources available online, how you can locate them and how to go about assessing their quality, you are in a position to start using them in your work. At this point, it becomes important for you understand and utilise one of the emerging referencing styles for online information. It is vital that you learn how to reference all of the sources you use in your work to help readers locate the resources that they might be interested in accessing themselves. Equally, unless you cite your online sources you will be as open to accusations of plagiarism as you would be if you had failed to cite the printed sources that you had used. This is particularly important because none of us develop ideas and arguments entirely free from the influence of the work of others. As such, ensuring that you follow a standard citation convention becomes extremely important to ensure you do not inadvertently plagiarise others' material.

> Legally, plagiarism has been defined as the act of appropriating the literary composition of another, or parts or passages of his/her writings, or language of the same, and passing them off as the product of one's own mind . . . [And] **ignorance, naiveté or sloppiness is no excuse**.
> (USM Social Science Guide to Plagiarism and Referencing,
> http://www.usm.maine.edu/~kuzma/Ideologies/Plagerism.
> html, accessed 7 July 2003, emphasis in the original)

When you utilise online information which you do not cite, not only are you liable to be accused of plagiarism but, just as with written material, you are liable to be in breach of copyright. International agreements of 'fair use' allow you to use copyrighted material without the author's written consent, but only as long as you cite the original source (for more information on copyright see: http://www.copyright.gov/).

The need to respect copyright and avoid plagiarism means that footnotes, references and citations are extremely important components in your academic work. Thus, to be on the safe side, whenever you use someone else's words within your own work, whether it be in the form of direct quotations, paraphrases or a heavy reliance on others' ideas, you must cite the original source.

## Basic citation standards

At present, there is no universal consensus on how to cite references from the Internet but the best advice is always to give as much information as possible. You should provide enough information that any future reader will be able to access the same information you have used or to be able to re-contact any organisation or newsgroup that you contacted during your research. One good method is to follow the same rules that have been developed for citing paper-based resources, whether by means of footnotes or of in-text referencing. Whatever format you use it is advisable to include the following elements: the name of the author, the title of the document, the name of the site, the URL, and either the date when you accessed the site, when it was first put on the web, or the date when it was last updated (Ó Dochartaigh 2002). Figures 4.1, 4.2 and 4.3 provide some examples of different Internet resources and give suggestions as to how they can be cited.

It should be pointed out that one of the key differences between the citation of online information and of more traditional sources is that in the former case there is no punctuation between sections. This is because most online addresses have their own internal

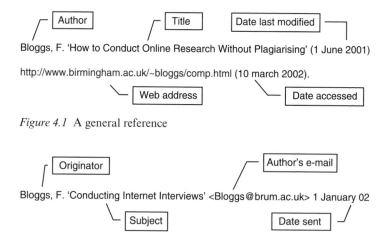

*Figure 4.1* A general reference

*Figure 4.2* Electronic mail

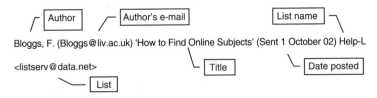

*Figure 4.3* A mailing list/newsgroup message

punctuation that would make any further punctuation confusing. Also, page numbers are almost never included when referencing online information. This is because most sites do not integrate page numbers and if you want to find a section of a site most web browsers have 'find' features which can pinpoint the quote or section. Similarly, when using printouts it might be impractical to list page numbers because different software packages tend to paginate documents differently.

While there are no hard rules governing the citation of online information, standards are emerging that you should make yourself aware of and follow (see: Citing Electronic Documentation, http://www.rhetoric.umn.edu/Student/Graduate/%7Emstewart/ citations/; Citing Sources and Avoiding Plagiarism, http://www.lib. duke.edu/libguide/citing.htm).

## Conclusion

Once you have found the information you are looking for, it becomes critical that you assess it for accuracy, authority and objectivity. This is particularly important for online resources. Not only is it possible for anyone to publish anything online, but few online documents ever receive the degree of external scrutiny that more traditional sources of information undergo. However, with a little practice you should be able to learn how to scan a site's URL for clues as to the quality of the information you can expect to find on the site, the type of server housing the site, and thus clues as to the type of bias you might expect to find.

We have seen that, going beyond the URL, there are many straightforward techniques to judge the quality of the information you find online. Not only is it possible to determine the type of document you are looking at, but it is also possible to determine the origin of a document, even if this requires you to access the site's domain registration information. Similarly, all sites include clues as to the authority, accuracy, currency and objectivity of the material they contain. As such, while the quality of online information varies from some of the best information available on a topic to some of the worst, most inaccurate and even misleading information you are likely to encounter, you should have the skills to begin judging whether you have a quality site or not.

Regardless of the quality of a site, it is always in your best interests to remember that the same rules governing any other information source hold true of Internet information. Thus, the same rules governing plagiarism and copyright infringement applicable to more traditional sources of information are equally applicable to online information. As such, you must learn to cite any of the online information that you use to inform your research.

# 5 Interactive research on the Internet

Other chapters in this book have provided you with details of information sources for politics and international relations that can be found on the Internet and have outlined ways of locating, evaluating and using web-based information. Additionally, the Internet can prove a valuable tool in conducting 'interactive' research, where the information you require is not stored in databases or archives but is to be found instead in people's responses to your questions. This type of research typically involves questionnaires, interviews and so forth. It is the kind of research that is highly relevant to study in areas such as politics and international relations, areas where values, opinions and preferences are always of great relevance. In this chapter we will consider some important issues when conducting this kind of research online.

## Why use the Internet?

From the researcher's perspective there are (as with any tool) advantages and disadvantages to using the Internet. On the positive side, the Internet provides a means by which researchers can identify and communicate with a vast number of individuals from across the world far more cheaply and quickly than they could using more conventional methods (Hewson *et al.* 2003). The Internet is also particularly useful for accessing certain kinds of information: it will be helpful, for example, if your project involves contacting particular political movements or social groups such as those with specialist interests or religious beliefs (Ó Dochartaigh 2002). The Internet may also be useful for exploring sensitive subjects where participants may only be comfortable airing their views online (Lee 2000). Participants may find it easier to express their own opinion online than they would in a face-to-face situation and the Internet can be used to preserve anonymity for particular groups. In addition, the Internet may allow you to gain access to groups that would not accept your participation in a face-to-face meeting (although the use of the Internet for such research may raise some problematic issues which are discussed further below). From the participant's perspective the use of the Internet may also have benefits. For example, responding to questions over the Internet may be more convenient for them than a face-to-face interview or group discussion. This may particularly be the case in asynchronous communication (i.e. communication over time) where they can respond to questions at their leisure. It can also help overcome problems of access, for example, for disabled people (Mann and Stewart 2000).

Having noted these various advantages to the Internet, it is worth also noting one limitation in terms of interactive research. Many do not have access to the Internet, particularly those in disadvantaged communities or in poorer parts of the world. In this sense, the community of Internet users to whom you will have access, although very large, is not necessarily a full cross-section of the population. This may or may not be significant depending on the nature of your particular research and the methods you are using but is always a point worth bearing in mind (Hewson *et al.* 2003).

## Defining the research question(s)

When conducting a piece of research at university it will sometimes be the case that you will be expected to decide for yourself the particular questions that you shall address. Where this is the case, there are a number of factors that are likely to influence your decision, such as your particular area of interest and what you have enjoyed most in your studies so far.

When deciding on your research question it is always advisable to think about why your chosen area of investigation is important: perhaps it builds, for example, on previous research, or aims to replicate some important findings; it might deal with a particularly topical issue or fill a gap in existing literature. Whatever it may be, it is useful to be clear about the rationale for the research that you are planning. Being clear on this will in turn allow you to be more specific about the particular research questions you need to be posing and what method will best suit your topic. You should also consider the feasibility of the research you wish to carry out and think about whether it is achievable in view of practical issues such as the time you have and the resources that are available to you.

## Choosing your research methods

Once you are clear about the questions you want to ask, it is important to think about the research methods appropriate to those questions. In very broad terms, two approaches may be identified which entail different research methods. On the one hand, some research is of a 'quantitative' sort, seeking objective, factual information concerning, most often, aspects of people's behaviour, from which generalisations can be made. On the other hand, more 'qualitative' research seeks to uncover the values, meanings and attitudes which underlie aspects of people's behaviour. These different approaches are sometimes thought of as standing in opposition to one another, being based on different 'epistemologies', or theories of knowledge. Those of a more 'positivist' outlook, who regard true knowledge as consisting of objective, verifiable facts, will tend to privilege the 'quantitative' approach, whilst those with a more 'interpretivist' outlook, who see the knowable world not in terms of pure objective fact but as something inevitably structured and informed by ideas and values, will tend to emphasise 'qualitative' research. This said, it may be that both sorts of research can make a contribution if they are carefully combined (Oakley 2000) In the end, which approach proves more important will depend upon your research question. If, for example, you are exploring changing patterns of voting preference during the life of a parliament, you will be looking for quantitative information about people's voting intentions which can be collated to show patterns of change over time. By contrast, if you are researching the conceptions and self-conceptions that underlie the experience of lone parents and how legislation affects their conduct, you will be looking for information of a more qualitative sort. Equally, different questions will call for different specific approaches. Those engaged in quantitative research will more often aim to choose their subjects randomly, in order for the research to be generalisable across the larger population. Those engaged in qualitative research will tend to use other sampling techniques, where gaining rich in-depth data from a small number of respondents is thought more important than statistical generalisation.

Many of the interactive research methods we are considering here become important in the context of more qualitative types of research, although some, particularly questionnaires, are also relevant to more quantitative investigations. In the section below, some of the research methods you can use online are discussed in order to help you identify the most appropriate for your research. For each method, practical considerations, such as time and resources, are outlined, and other advantages and disadvantages of each approach are summarised. In general, traditional research methods can, with small but important modifications, be adapted to suit online environments. Although, some believe that completely new methods will develop as we gain greater experience of online environments (Hine 2000).

Whichever method you use, you need to locate participants for your research. If you are not using key informants to provide you with details of people to contact, two possible strategies are to locate people through e-mail mailing lists or to access online discussions. There are various different types of e-mail mailing lists; some are unidirectional and are used as a way of disseminating information (e.g. about new books or events), others are created for interaction between members and vary between being moderated and un-moderated. You can search for specific mailing lists through search engines such as Topica (http://lists.topica.com) or meta-list.net (http://www.meta-list.net). Once you have located relevant e-mail lists it is important to evaluate their appropriateness to your research. You might, for example, seek to weed out lists that are only open to invited members or those where the discussion is very slow with few contributors (Ó Dochartaigh 2002).

You could also locate online discussion groups that are based around your topic. To revisit briefly some of the discussion in chapter 3, there are two main types of online discussion sites – newsgroups and web forums – which differ from e-mail mailing lists in the way you post and read messages and the way in which these discussions are archived. The majority of newsgroups are on Usenet and you can tell what the newsgroup is about by looking at its name. The name is organised hierarchically and there are seven standard newsgroup categories to provide you with an idea of what the discussion is about, for example, **rec** is for recreational, **biz** is for business and **soc** is for social affairs. Further categories provide you with more information about a particular group; therefore a newsgroup with the name 'rec.music.pop' tells you that the newsgroup falls within the recreational category, is about music, and is specifically about pop music (Lee 2000). One important factor to note is whether the groups you find are entirely open or more regulated, as this may effect what you make of the material you find there. You can search for newsgroups either by group or by individual messages on a number of search engines. The second type of online discussion, a web forum, is typically a web-based discussion set up to debate the content of the website from which the forum is linked. These discussions can often be linked to topical debates and can be located through search engines (Ó Dochartaigh 2002).

Once you have selected your mailing list or online discussion there are a number of ways you can go about contacting individuals to take part in your questionnaire, interview or focus-group study. For example, you could send a message to everyone on the list, or, if the list or online discussion is managed, you could contact the head of the list or moderator first. Further discussion about contacting individuals is contained in the discussions on particular research methods below.

One further issue to consider at the outset is whether an online approach is suitable given the particular group you may be wanting to contact. Clearly it will be suitable where the target group is likely to have regular access to e-mail and some technical competence. However, if members of the target group are less likely to have access and competence, you will clearly find it more difficult to generate a sample of respondents, and the sample you do generate may be less than fully representative. Where this is the case, it may be necessary to supplement your online research with more traditional face-to-face or paper-based methods.

### Questionnaires

It is appropriate to use a questionnaire or survey when you wish to gain information from a large number of people but do not require the more in-depth, detailed information that can be gained from interviews or focus groups. Questionnaires are particularly useful if you wish to conduct statistical analysis as they typically contain fixed, structured questions that will yield responses that are straightforward to analyse.

The two main ways of delivering the questionnaire to potential participants are either directly via e-mail or by using a web-based survey. Which one of these you decide to use is likely to depend on your own technical ability and the characteristics, including the technical competence, of the group you are trying to reach (Mann and Stewart 2000). The approach you choose will influence the design of the questionnaire. Some of the basic design principles applicable to paper-based questionnaires apply also to Internet versions. Most of all, they should be easy for respondents to complete. To this end, they should be logical in terms of topic and questions of the same format should be placed together. The format of a questionnaire should include an introductory explanatory paragraph, and as far as possible it should be easy, non-threatening and should not require very long answers. Finally, you should try to ensure that each question fits on a page and that the spacing is appropriate (Anderson 1998).

When sending the questionnaire to participants via e-mail one of the simplest ways is to send them an exact copy of a paper-based version as an attachment that they can fill out on screen and return via e-mail. Alternatively, you could send the questions simply in the form of an e-mail. These options are desirable if your participants are not likely to have a high degree of technical skill. However, opening and returning an attachment may be off-putting to some respondents and formatting the e-mail in the second option could be difficult (Mann and Stewart 2000). The use of web-based survey programs can overcome these problems. These are programs which organise the data as it is entered and respond to the entries made. There are a number of these programs freely available on the web. They can also help you develop the questionnaire so as to make it easier and faster for users to fill in, for example, by the use of drop-down boxes or by tailoring the program so that parts of the questionnaire which are not relevant to certain participants can be hidden to the user. The use of a survey program also makes data collection far easier: you will have none of the inputting errors that can arise when using paper-based questionnaires, as the data has already been entered directly by the participants (Mann and Stewart 2000).

Once you have designed your questionnaire, you will need to think about how you can contact potential participants and persuade them to take part in your study. The most direct method is to contact potential individuals directly via e-mail, either with your questionnaire attached or with a link to the website where your survey is based. No method is perfect, however, and there are some potential drawbacks to this approach. First, a probability sample can be difficult to generate as there is no single directory containing the e-mail addresses of all Internet users, and those that exist are incomplete and likely to be out of date. This is a limitation if you are seeking a real cross-section of people, but less of a problem if you are exploring a particular group or institution. Also, e-mailing people directly may be thought by some to be a nuisance and you may be accused of 'spamming' (Hewson *et al.* 2003). For this reason, you need to be diplomatic in the way you approach potential respondents. Alternatively, you might seek to avoid this problem by contacting the head of a discussion list to ask for their help as a gatekeeper (Witmer *et al.* 1999). Another method of gaining respondents is to set up a website to tell people about the project and then put the details of the project on search engines (Harris 1996). However, a potential problem with this approach is the difficulty of identifying the sampling frame: for example, you cannot measure the number and the characteristics of the people who saw the advertisements for the project and did not take part. How significant this problem is largely depends on the particular nature of your research project and how much it matters about identifying reasons for non-response. Certainly, e-mailing people directly with the questionnaire provides you with more control and a greater idea of non-response rates. Finally, one way of increasing the scope of your survey is through 'snowball sampling', where you contact a number of respondents directly and ask them to forward the questionnaire to people they know. Of course, if you use this technique for a piece of research where you are seeking respondents with particular characteristics, you need to be clear in your communications as to the kind of respondents that you are looking for.

Response rates to e-mail surveys have declined over the past fifteen years. This trend may be due, ironically, to the very prevalence of Internet use today. Fifteen years ago the majority of people online were technology enthusiasts who were keen to respond to things like online questionnaires. Today, the Internet is more widely used and the people who use it are more discriminating about how they use it. Further, the increasing amounts of junk mail individuals receive and the threat of viruses combine to make response to questionnaires less frequent (Sheehan 2001). In view of this, you may need to be more proactive in encouraging participation. You might, in your posting, stress the importance and relevance of your research, or alternatively provide incentives such as money or prizes to take part (Mann and Stewart 2000). Another way of increasing the likelihood of participation is to contact potential respondents in advance, in writing or by telephone, so they do not simply delete your questionnaire when it comes.

### Interviews

The interview is a popular qualitative research technique and can be a rich source of information. Advantages of using online interviews, as opposed to the more traditional variety, include the access you have to a greater number of people and a potentially higher response rate, as it may be more convenient for individuals to take part online (Selwyn and Robson 1998). However, as with online questionnaires, you may need to be imaginative in finding ways to persuade people who don't know you to participate (Harris 1996).

There are three main types of interview: structured, semi-structured and unstructured. Within these categories, a distinction can also be made between respondent interviews where the interviewer maintains control and informant interviews where the emphasis is on interviewees' responses (Powney and Watts 1987). A very structured interview is likely to produce information similar to that which you could gain from a questionnaire, whereas unstructured interviews can be used to obtain more detailed information; although, as interviews of this sort are more time consuming, you are unlikely to gain information from as large a sample as is possible with questionnaires. Here, the discussion will focus on semi-structured interviews.

When designing your interview schedule, there are a series of components that you should normally include. The first is an introduction, where you can provide a brief overview of your project and what you would like to talk to the interviewee about. The second is a warm-up section that typically involves easy, descriptive and non-controversial questions. The third part is the main body of your interview, where it is advisable to leave any risky or difficult questions until last, just in case the respondent stops answering or becomes uncomfortable. The final section incorporates a 'cool-off' component: a few questions at the end to draw the interview to a close, perhaps asking the interviewee if they have anything else to add or questions to ask, and thanking them for their time.

One factor you need to consider that may affect the reliability and validity of the results that you obtain is whether the questions are understood in the same way by the participant as they are by the researcher (Shipman 1997). To minimise problems here, try to avoid questions that are very long or involve jargon when preparing your schedule. You should also, for obvious reasons, avoid questions that are leading or biased. These considerations are particularly important when asking questions online, as participants in this setting do not have other signals, such as non-verbal communication, to help them understand what you mean.

It is also worth bearing in mind that in text-based communication there are symbolic ways in which you can help ensure that your thoughts get across, for example by using symbols to indicate a joke (Selwyn and Robson 1998). A further issue in interviews is that participants may not always tell the truth; they may lie, for example, in order to avoid personal questions, to hide ignorance or to avoid embarrassment (Shipman 1997). In a face-to-face interview, you may find these situations easier to identify through non-verbal signals. It is more difficult in online interviews, and so it is important in these contexts that you analyse carefully the responses you get for any signs of inconsistency or evasion on the part of interviewees. Whilst there are added issues of this sort in online interviews, it is equally the case that in some ways the lack of non-verbal communication can be beneficial. The participant is less likely to be influenced by any unintentional bias on the part of the interviewer, such as may be expressed, for example, through tone of voice (Harris 1996). Further, as the interaction is not face-to-face, people may actually feel more comfortable giving full and honest responses.

Interviews can be done in real-time or over a period (Hewson *et al.* 2003). If conducting the interview over a period of time you also need to decide whether you should stagger questions or send the whole schedule to the participant at once. Staggered questionnaires are sometimes advantageous because, although some people may drop out before the process is complete, they provide greater opportunity for the interviewer to ask for clarification or pose supplementary questions that lead to more thoughtful answers (Mann and Stewart 2000). Particularly when you are interviewing someone in real-time, think carefully beforehand about how you would probe further in order to encourage an interviewee to expand on what they have said. One problem in online interviewing is that it can be particularly difficult to determine whether a short answer has been given because that is all the participant has to say on a topic, or whether it is because they do not really wish to answer the question fully. It is therefore a good idea to consider how you would use prompts to encourage answers from the interviewee and to ensure they have said as much as they are able. You should also reflect as you go along on the way you are asking the questions and the content of those questions, making revisions where necessary in the early stages of the research (Jones 1991).

The quality of the data collected in an interview may be enhanced if there is a good rapport between interviewer and interviewee. Generating a rapport may be more difficult online than in face-to-face interviews but there are techniques that you can use. You might preface the interview by discussing some common interest, or raising an issue that you know is of particular interest to the interviewee (Jones 1991). If the interviewee has met you before in a face-to-face environment, you might remind them of this or you might mention a common acquaintance – the interviewee may be someone recommended to you by your supervisor, for example. Whilst it may be a little harder to develop rapport online, in certain situations online interviews can overcome difficulties of face-to-face interviewing: for example, in face-to-face situations people can make judgments about you on the basis of age, gender or race that may influence the discussion. As the characteristics of participants in online discussions are not so obvious it screens out the effects of preconceptions or prejudices (Selwyn and Robson 1998).

### *Focus groups*

Focus groups, like interviews, can be a rich source of in-depth information on a particular topic. When people talk in a group it can enhance recall and may also help you to explore a range of viewpoints more quickly than you could in one-to-one interviews. By using the Internet you can bring together a group of people who may be interested in a particular topic but are geographically dispersed making a face-to-face meeting difficult. It may also be the case that the nature of the topic means that people are more comfortable discussing it online in an anonymous environment. Again, some threats to validity and reliability should be considered in the preparation and conducting of the focus group, and guidelines for face-to-face focus groups can be applied to the online situation.

As with all online methods you need to consider how you are going to recruit your participants, whether through e-mailing people directly, through snowball sampling or by contacting newsgroups for interested individuals. You also need to consider the composition of your focus group; for example, the age and sex of participants and whether they know one another (at least online) or are strangers. While it is desirable that the group has something in common, using a pre-existing group may not be ideal because discussion between people who are familiar with one another's views is more likely to proceed along entrenched lines. Also, in a pre-existing group, responses may be affected where participants are worried about what their friends or peers think (Anderson 1998). Sometimes, however, the use of a pre-existing group is unavoidable: if your focus group is concerned with very specific area, for example, you may well find individuals who are used to holding discussions with one another online as they are all members of the same newsgroup. While not ideal, these contexts can sometimes bring advantages if participants feel more at home in familiar company. Again, the importance of these kinds of factors is likely to depend upon the particular topic you are researching.

More generally, also, the use of online groups has advantages and disadvantages. There is always a possibility when using online groups that some participants in the group are not who they say they are (this is discussed further in the analysis section below). This said, a lack of knowledge of the identities of the individuals involved can sometimes be beneficial. This is because possible problems arising from perceived hierarchies in the group (as a result, for example, of differences in gender and age) which may occur in a face-to-face environment can be avoided. The size of the group may also be important. As a guideline, in face-to-face environments six to twelve participants are typically used, although three to five can be used if the topic needs to be explored in great depth (Anderson 1998). Your decision may also partly be determined by the number of people you feel you could moderate well, and if you are using real-time discussion or not.

This takes us to the further consideration as to whether you are going to organise your focus group on a synchronous or an asynchronous basis. A synchronous arrangement involves immediate, 'conversational' discussion, along the lines of an Internet chat room. These environments clearly have more in common with face-to-face communication, but can sometimes be slightly difficult for participants to follow and they will need good computer skills in order to take part. An asynchronous arrangement involves participants receiving and sending e-mail messages and allows time to consider what is being said before making a contribution. This arrangement is more ordered and straightforward and is more suitable if some members of the group are not particularly IT literate – although it is worth bearing in mind that the nature of the discussion will change, as people have more time to think about answers and it will lose the immediacy of a direct, conversational discussion (Mann and Stewart 2000).

As with online interviews, your rapport with the group is also important in terms both of encouraging positive participation and of resolving problems amicably. A good rapport may help the researcher, for example, when facing difficulties of dealing with dominant individuals within the group and may also help to encourage quieter members (Gunter 2000). How easy it proves to develop a rapport will depend on your prior experience of moderating online focus groups, the participants' prior experience of using the technology, and your relationship with the individuals taking part – whether, for example, you have communicated with them before or have met them face-to-face (Baym 1995 cited in Mann and Stewart 2000: 129). In any case, as we noted previously, there will always be conversational gambits that you can use to help build up a rapport (see the section on interviews above).

You also need to think carefully in advance about the questions you are going to ask and how you are going to ask them. It is usually advisable to develop in advance a schedule of fairly open questions for the participants to discuss. This type of approach has advantages similar to those associated with the semi-structured interview discussed above – for example, by using a pre-prepared list of open questions, the analysis of the data is easier as comparisons between the responses of different groups may be made (Gunter 2000).

### *Observation*

Online, you have the opportunity to observe and understand a vast array of virtual communities. There are two main types of observation: participant observation and direct observation. As the terms suggest, the difference between the two lies in the degree to which you, the observer, participate in the group that you are studying. In each case, you can also engage in overt observation, openly observing groups with the participants' consent, or covert observation, where you can hide your identity from the participants.

The type of observation you opt for will have implications for your research. For example, if you make a decision to observe overtly, it is likely that your presence will have some effect on the behaviour of individuals in the group, as they know that they are being studied. On the other hand, this form of observation does allow you to question the group, to ask for clarification and to prompt further insights. In addition, ethically, you are in a stronger position as you will be able to agree terms of access and means of ensuring confidentiality with the group. Covert observation can take different forms. You can 'lurk', making no contribution to the discussion, or you can act as an ordinary participant in the group if you feel this is important to understanding what is going on. There is clearly an advantage in covert observation in that you are less likely to influence the behaviour of participants. On the other hand, you will not be able to ask for clarification on aspects you do not fully understand. Further, ethically, this is potentially a far more problematic form of investigation and care needs to be taken. We shall return to this point below.

Observation online can clearly reduce your workload, overcoming the need to travel and to organise gatherings of the group. It is worth noting, however, that if you are using a pre-existing group, then getting to know the group, researching its history and gaining an understanding of its rules of behaviour are all things over which you will need to take time. It is very important when using focus group material that you know the group context well enough so as not simply to lift the data out of context when analysing it (Thomsen *et al.* 1998).

## Ethical considerations

The ethical considerations surrounding face-to-face research also apply to research on the Internet and you should consider the potential ethical issues involved at the beginning of your project (Bassey 1999). Two particularly important issues to consider are those of informed consent and confidentiality.

Gaining informed consent in an online environment may be more complex than in the face-to-face situation. It can take more time, as it may require more discussions via e-mail in order to ensure that participants understand what they are agreeing to. E-mail exchanges of this sort may put participants off seeking clarification or asking all the questions they wish about the research and it will be more difficult for you to ensure that the participant fully understands what they are agreeing to than it might be in a face-to-face encounter (Mann and Stewart 2000). It is therefore especially important to be clear to participants and to provide additional information if you think that they have not fully grasped the process. Also, when studying a virtual community, it is sometimes very difficult to gain consent from the entire community, particularly as the composition of the group may sometimes change over the period of the research (Lee 2000). It is therefore advisable to check periodically during your research that everyone involved is clear about the arrangement.

You also need to be aware of any risk that your participants might come to some form of harm as a result of your project and to think about how any such risks can be minimised. Do not underestimate the possibility of particular problems arising. For example, in online group discussions a participant may be insulted or harassed by other group members for having different views. In some cases, even contacting potential participants or probing too deeply when interviewing could cause distress. You can try and reduce risks here by highlighting to participants at the beginning of group discussions the very public nature of what they are writing. You might also emphasise the fact that all are entitled to express their views within the parameters of the expected 'netiquette' (see chapter 2). Finally, you can allow participants a 'get-out clause' should they decide that they simply do not want to answer your questions or participate further in discussion. For example, you could ensure that individuals felt they could withdraw at any time by placing a withdraw button that was clearly visible to participants enabling them to exit the research (Hewson *et al.* 2003).

A further important issue with respect to interactive research is that of confidentiality. You should make every attempt to keep the identity of each participant confidential and, where you are engaging with subjects overtly, make it clear to participants exactly how that confidentiality will be maintained when the results of the research are written up (Anderson 1998). When preparing your research you should consider how secure the information is that is sent between you and your participants and how you will conceal the identity and e-mail addresses of the individuals taking part in the discussion (Mann and Stewart 2000). There are questions of balance here. It may seem desirable to keep the identities of all participants completely confidential; however, this can equally limit the value of the research, making it difficult for others to evaluate or replicate the work.

Further, it is generally hard in online contexts to make a clear distinction between what is private and what is public space. In some areas, such as e-mail, this is straightforward, but for online discussions it is not so clear cut (Lee 2000). This question is particularly problematic when publishing findings from covert observation of a discussion. The decisions that you make on these issues will be shaped by your research, but always treat participants with the utmost respect. The Internet makes these ethical considerations more difficult and specific guidelines are scarce. If you cannot decide on a particular issue, try thinking about it from the participant's point of view and ask the opinions of others, including your supervisor.

## Analysis of data

How you analyse your data will depend largely on whether you have used more quantitative methods (such as questionnaires) or more qualitative ones (such as interviews, focus groups or observation).

Quantitative data is analysed by means of various statistical tests that can be used to describe themes or relationships and to support or reject hypotheses that were set out at the beginning of the study. If you are going to use any statistical test you should decide which one you are going to use before you begin designing your instruments and collecting data. This is because you have to design your study with the statistical test in mind. You need, for example, to consider the number of responses required to make the test you have chosen appropriate, and whether the data you collect will provide all the information you need to carry out the analysis.

When analysing qualitative data, such as interviews and focus groups, one approach involves looking for meaningful patterns or themes in the data. This approach is particularly appropriate if you have developed semi-structured schedules for the research, as this will have encouraged similar coverage of questions by respondents and so analysing the data will be easier than it would be with an unstructured interview (Patton 1990). Text of responses can be coded into themes, either by hand, using highlighters and/ or scissors and glue, or with the help of a computer package that will identify patterns. In the context of an online discussion you may also tally the number of postings on particular themes. These may also be indexed against the characteristics of contributors, if known (see Thomsen *et al.* 1998). An examination of content may also provide an insight into how the members of the group use the online discussions as a process of communication (see Postmes *et al.* 1998). In general, you must take care when analysing data not lose the overall context of the interview or discussion. Since qualitative data is not susceptible to the same sort of exhaustive numerical analysis as quantitative data, it is wise to read this kind of material a number of times in order to pick up on all its patterns and themes.

As a general rule when analysing the data you must think carefully about the quality of the data you have collected and think about how it differs to the same method in a face-to-face environment. Finally, when you go 'into the field' you may find that you encounter difficulties that you did not expect. In these situations, make a note of them (do not ignore them) and write about them when you are analysing the data. Few pieces of research are entirely problem-free and where you do encounter difficulties it is always best to be honest about them and discuss them in your final report – this will strengthen, not detract from, your analysis (Mann and Stewart 2000).

## Interactive online learning

Whilst the principal focus of this book is researching online, it is worth saying something briefly about another use to which Internet technology is increasingly being put in Higher Education. Most students are now likely to have some exposure during their programme of study to interactive learning packages, generally known as Virtual Learning Environments (VLEs). These software packages allow the interactive learning process to continue outside the classroom or lecture theatre and are generally used to supplement those more traditional learning contexts (although they have become a central element in 'distance learning' programmes).

There are now a range of such packages available and they vary in terms of their particular facilities. However, there are some general features which most share. VLEs are designed to provide a means of online communication and access to materials for staff and students on a particular module. Typically, they provide a site which students can access and on to which module teachers can post useful information including reading lists, lecture and seminar schedules and other documents such as lecture notes, handouts, style guides, sample essays and so forth. They will generally also contain a facility for message posting so that the module teacher can communicate easily with the students and ensure they remain fully up to date. A well as supplying an additional line of communication, these facilities mean that students can engage in more directed pre-class preparation, thereby allowing more time in class for fruitful discussion between well-prepared participants. Aside from supporting in-class interaction, however, VLEs are also designed to provide an additional means of interaction outside the classroom. They generally incorporate facilities for e-mail-based discussion, so that students can discuss the topics studied on the module with their fellow students and with the teacher. This facility also allows students to post queries and to raise questions which otherwise they may find themselves struggling with alone. Finally, these packages also allow module teachers to post up links to useful Internet sites that students can follow as they work their way through a module, thereby helping them keep up with topical events of relevance and also helping introduce them to the kind of Internet research that is the main focus of this book.

How much use a VLE proves to be may often depend upon the nature and requirements of the particular module, and the technology cannot be regarded as a complete substitute for the experience of traditional face-to-face learning and teaching. It is also arguable that we should beware becoming too beguiled by the technology, that we should take care to ensure that learning and teaching is supported by, rather than determined by, the technology (Lee 2003). That said, with appropriate training and care in use, there can be little doubt that VLEs augment the learning experience and we are likely see a lot more of them in future.

## Conclusion

So much of politics is concerned with shaping, managing, articulating or responding to values, opinions and perceptions; and in view of this, interactive forms of research may well prove relevant to your studies. This chapter has provided you with a brief outline of some of the ways in which you can use the Internet as an interactive research tool. You will have to decide the methods that are right for your research. Using the Internet as a research tool may yield some interesting research findings, and may also provide you with an opportunity to make a contribution to the debate in your field. It is still a very new area, and other new technologies such as video conferencing, which have not been discussed here, are starting to be used, although, as yet, few students are likely to have access to the advanced (and expensive) technology required. We have not had the space here to go into great detail about all the tools and methods we have discussed. If you would like to explore any or all of these areas in more detail, you could start with the extra reading provided below.

## Extra reading

Hewson, C., Yule, P., Laurent, D. and Vogel, C. (2003) *Internet Research Methods: A Practical Guide for the Social and Behavioural Sciences*, London: Sage.

Mann, C. and Stewart, F. (2000) *Internet Communication and Qualitative Research: A Handbook for Researching Online*, London: Sage.

Ó Dochartaigh, N. (2002) *The Internet Research Handbook: A Practical Guide for Students and Researchers in the Social Sciences*, London: Sage.

# 6  Conclusion

There can be no doubt that for students of politics and international relations, the Internet constitutes a resource of great potential value. Sites concerned with some aspect of politics are amongst the most common and provide a huge amount of information, argument, comment and opinion. At the same time, as we have seen, the great strengths of the Internet can also sometimes be potential weaknesses: its sheer size can mean that one is overwhelmed and its openness can mean that the material to be found there is sometimes of little value. With these points in mind, this book has aimed to provide advice that will enable you, with practice, to become an effective and discerning user of the Internet: effective in being able to search quickly and efficiently for the kind of information that will help you in your studies; discerning in being able to evaluate the content of sites that you find and to think critically about their origin, purpose and intended audience. If you are able to develop and combine these two crucial abilities, you will find the Internet an extremely useful tool.

It is also important that you always remember that the Internet is just a tool. It should always be your servant and never your master. To this end, always bear in mind that the Internet is never the only learning source you have, and may rarely be the main one: books, periodicals, newspapers and, of course, the classroom remain indispensable to your learning and the Internet is good only to the extent that it integrates with and supports your studies more generally. So if the Internet proves inadequate for a particular piece of research that you are engaged in, leave it behind and concentrate on other resources. Similarly, when producing work, do not let the Internet dictate your style. Because of the ease with which material can be published online it often lacks the scholarly style and depth of argument that is expected in academic work, unlike books or journal articles which have been through more rigorous assessment and editorial processes. So it is important that you have these other, more considered models to learn from. If you keep these considerations in mind, you should be better positioned to ensure that the Internet is a resource that helps rather than hinders you in meeting the expectations of your programme of study.

To a large extent, of course, how quickly and easily you are able to develop effective and discerning use of the Internet and to integrate it into your work at university will depend on your prior experience of the medium. These days, many students embarking on their studies are already quite familiar with the use of computers and have some experience with the Internet – many, but by no means all. Students constitute a more diverse community than was once the case, coming from diverse educational and social backgrounds and different parts of the world. In this context, experience with Internet technology is bound to vary. Universities recognise this and so now generally offer support and guidance in computer use. This provision is well worth taking of advantage of if you have little experience with the technology, or even if you just feel you need a refresher course. Equally, the speed with which computers and the Internet have come to prominence in academic life means that those who have been working in universities for any length of time have themselves had to adapt quickly to the new technology and will generally be well placed to understand how challenging it can be. So, whether it is a matter of how to go about finding information, how to judge whether a particular site is appropriate, or how to present your findings, don't be afraid to ask. Beyond this, the key to using the Internet to the greatest benefit is, as with all aspects of your studies, perseverance.

# Appendix
## List of useful websites

The number of Internet sites is immense and constantly growing. It is also constantly changing as particular sites come and go. As a result, there is always a risk that any list of useful sites will become outdated even before it is published. In order to minimise this problem, we have limited our list for the most part to sites provided by larger and more reputable organisations. What follows, therefore, is a collection of sites that are likely to be relatively permanent and of particular interest to students of politics and international relations. We have also limited the list to sites that are open access and available in English.

In order to avoid an excessively long list, in the case of government and international organisation sites, we have only listed the main homepage, from which you can then easily navigate to more particular sites. For example, the listing for UK government is http://www.directgov.uk. From here you can follow links to sites for the main government departments (such as the Treasury or the Ministry of Defence), for government information sources (such as the Met Office or the Office of National Statistics), for government agencies (such as the Financial Services Authority or the Commission for Racial Equality), and for many other related sites, from the Monarchy to the Social Exclusion Unit.

### Government

British Government – http://www.directgov.uk
British Local Government – http://www.local.gov.uk
British Parliament – http://www.parliament.uk

Northern Ireland Assembly – http://www.niassembly.gov.uk
Scottish Parliament – http://www.scottish.parliament.uk
US Congress – http://www.congress.org
US Government – http://www.firstgov.gov
Welsh Assembly – http://www.wales.gov.uk

## Political parties

British National Party – http://www.bnp.org.uk
Conservative Party – http://www.conservative-party.org.uk
Democratic Unionist Party – http://www.dup.org.uk
Federation of European Green Parties – http://
   www.europeangreens.org
Green Party – http://www.greenparty.org.uk
Labour Party – http://www.labour.org.uk
Liberal Democrats – http://www.libdems.org.uk
Natural Law Party – http://www.natural-law-party.org.uk
Party of European Socialists – http://www.eurosocialists.org
Plaid Cymru – http://www.plaidcymru.org
Political Parties World Wide Links – http://www.gksoft.com/govt
Scottish Nationalists – http://www.snp.org.uk
Sinn Fein – http://www.sinnfein.ie
Social Democratic and Labour Party – http://www.sdlp.ie
Socialist Workers Party – http://www.swp.org.uk
UK Independence Party – http://www.ukip.org
Ulster Unionists – http://www.uup.org
US Democratic Party – http://www.democrats.org
US Republican Party – http://www.rnc.org

## International organisations

Association of Southeast Asian Nations – http://
   www.aseansec.org
British Council – http://wwwbritcoun.org
The Commonwealth – http://www.thecommonwealth.org
Council of Europe – http://www.coe.int
European Central Bank – http://www.ecb.int
European Court of Human Rights – http://www.echr.coe.int
European Union – http://europa.eu.int

G8 Information Centre – http://www.g8.utoronto.ca
International Court of Justice – http://www.icj-cij.org
International Criminal Court – http://www.icc-cpi.int
International Labour Organization – http://www.ilo.org
International Monetary Fund – http://www.imf.org
Inter-Parliamentary Union – http://www.ipu.org
Interpol – http://www.interpol.int
League of Arab States – http://www.arableagueonline.org
NATO – http://www.nato.int
Organization of American States – http://www.oas.org
Organisation for Economic Co-operation and Development – http://www.oecd.org
Organization of Petroleum Exporting Countries – http://www.opec.org
Organization for Security and Co-operation in Europe – http://www.osce.org
ReliefWeb – http://www.reliefweb.int
South Asian Association for Regional Co-operation – http://www.saarc-sec.org
Union of International Associations – http://www.uia.org
United Nations – http://www.un.org
Western European Union – http://www.weu.int
World Bank – http://www.worldbank.org
World Health Organization – http://www.who.int
World Trade Organization – http://www.wto.org

## Pressure groups

Amnesty International – http://www.amnesty.org
Charter 88 – http://www.charter88.org.uk
Child Poverty Action Group – http://www.cpag.org.uk
Confederation of British Industry – http://www.cbi.org.uk
Electoral Reform Society – http://www.electoral-reform.org.uk
Friends of the Earth – http://www.foe.co.uk
Greenpeace – http://www.greenpeace.org
Jubilee 2000 – http://www.jubilee2000.org/jubilee2000
Liberty – http://www.liberty-human-rights.org.uk
Trades Union Congress – http://www.tuc.org.uk

**Think tanks**

Adam Smith Institute – http://www.adamsmith.org
Brookings Institution – http://www.brook.edu
Cato Institute – http://www.cato.org
Centre for Policy Studies – http://www.cps.org.uk
Centre for Strategic and International Studies – http://www.csis.org
Demos – http://www.demos.co.uk
Fabian Society – http://www.fabian-society.org.uk
Fawcett Society – http://www.fawcettsociety.org.uk
Heritage Foundation – http://www.heritage.org
Institute for Economic Affairs – http://www.iea.org.uk
Institute of Fiscal Studies – http://www.ifs.org.uk
Institute for Public Policy Research – http://www.ippr.org.uk
International Institute for Strategic Studies – http://www.iiss.org
Labour Research Department – http://www.lrd.org.uk
NIRA Directory of Think Tanks – http://www.nira.go.jp/ice
Royal Institute of International Affairs – http://www.riia.org
Social Market Foundation – http://www.smf.co.uk

**Broadcast media**

BBC – http://www.bbc.co.uk
Broadcasting Standards Commission – http://www.ofcom.org.uk
CBS – http://www.cbs.com
Channel 4 – http://www.channel4.com
CNN – http://www.cnn.com
ITV – http://www.itv.com
Media UK – http://www.mediauk.com
MSNBC – http://www.msnbc.com
National Public Radio – http://www.npr.org
NBC – http://www.nbc.com
Newspapers.Com – http://newspapers.com
Pandia Newsfinder – http://www.pandia.com/news
Sky TV – http://www.sky.com

## Newspapers and magazines

Alternative News Centre – http://www.altpress.org
The Daily Telegraph – http://www.telegraph.co.uk
The Economist – http://www.economist.com
The Financial Times – http://www.ft.com
The Guardian – http://www.guardian.co.uk
The Independent – http://www.independent.co.uk
International Herald Tribune – http://www.iht.com
London Review of Books – http://www.lrb.co.uk
The Morning Star – http://www.morningstaronline.co.uk
The New Statesman – http://www.newstatesman.com
New York Review of Books – http://www.nybooks.com
The New York Times – http://www.nyt.com
News Now – http://www.newsnow.com
Newspapers Online – http://www.newspapers.com
Newsweek – http://www.newsweekeurope.com
The Observer – http://observer.guardian.co.uk
Press Complaints Commission – http://www.pcc.org.uk
Prospect – http://www.prospect-magazine.co.uk
Red Pepper – http://www.redpepper.org.uk
Reuters News Agency – http://www.reuters.co.uk
Searchlight – http://www.s-light.demon.co.uk
The Spectator – http://www.spectator.co.uk
The Sunday Times – http://www.timesonline.co.uk
Time Magazine – http://www.time.com/time
The Times – http://www.timesonline.co.uk
UKPOL Online Magazine – http://www.ukpol.co.uk
The Washington Post – http://www.washingtonpost.com

## Libraries

British Library – http://www.bl.uk
COPAC (UK University Library Catalogues) – http://
    www.copac.ac.uk
The European Library – http://www.theeuropeanlibrary.org
Global Library for Critical Social Science – http://
    www.theglobalsite.ac.uk
Internet Public Library – http://www.ipl.org

Library Index – http://www.libdex.com

LibrarySpot (online libraries) – http://www.libraryspot.com

LIBWEB (comprehensive international index) – http://lists.webjunction.org/libweb

National Library of Scotland – http://www.nls.uk

National Library of Wales – http://www.llgc.org.uk

Net Library – http://www.netlibrary.com

US Library of Congress – http://www.loc.gov


## Major directories and gateways

Archives Hub (gateway to university archives) – http://www.archiveshub.ac.uk

Argus Clearinghouse – http://www.clearinghouse.net

British Columbia Political Resources – http://www.library.ubc.ca/poli

BUBL UK Information Service – http://www.bubl.ac.uk

Cata-list – http://www.lsoft.com/lists.listref.html

Council of European Social Science Date Archives – http://www.nsd.uib.no/cessda

DiplomaticNet – http://www.diplomaticnet.com

Facsnet Expert Finder – http://www.facsnet.org

Global Yellow Pages – http://globalyp.com/world.htm

Google Group Directory – http://groups-beta.google.com

Governments on the WWW – http://www.gksoft.com/govt

ICQ e-mail lookup – http://www.icq.com/whitepages

Infomine – http://infomine.ucr.edu

Invisible Web – http://www.profusion.com

Invisible Web Directory – http://www.invisible-web.net

JISC Resource Guides – http://www.jisc.ac.uk/resourceguides

Keele Political Science Resources – http://www.psr.keele.ac.uk

Librarian's Index – http://lii.org

List Universe – http://tile.net/lists

Looksmart – http://www.search.looksmart.com

Mailing List Gurus – http://lists.gurus.com

National Digital Archive of Datasets – http://www.ndad.ulcc.ac.uk

Open Directory – http://www.dmoz.org

PeopleSearch – http://www.peoplesearch.net

Political Information – http://www.politicalinformation.com
Political Resources on the Net – http://www.politicalresources.net
Politics Online – http://www.politicsonline.com
Search Engine Guide – http://www.searchengineguide.com
Searchability – http://www.searchability.com
Social Science Information Gateway – http://www.sosig.ac.uk
Top Ten – http://www.toptenlinks.com
Topica – http://lists.topica.com
University of Michigan Documents Center – http://
    www.lib.umich.edu/govdoc/polisci.html
UK Data Archive – http://www.data-archive.ac.uk
Web of Knowledge – http://wok.mimas.ac.uk
Yahoo – http://www.yahoo.com

## Other

American Political Science Association – http://www.apsanet.org
British International Studies Association – http://www.bisa.ac.uk
Census Information – http://www.census.ac.uk
Census Information (US) – http://www.census.gov
Citizens Advice Bureaux – http://www.nacab.org.uk
Economic and Social Research Council – http://www.esrc.ac.uk
Equal Opportunities Commission – http://www.eoc.org.uk
European Consortium for Political Research http://
    www.essex.ac.uk/ecpr
Gallup Polls – http://www.gallup.com
Higher Education Academy Centre for Learning and Teaching:
    Sociology, Anthropology and Politics – http://
    www. c-sap.bham.ac.uk
Higher Education Funding Council for England – http://
    www.hefce.ac.uk
Higher Education Funding Council for Wales – http://
    www.wfc.ac.uk
Higher Education and Research Opportunities UK – http://
    www.hero.ac.uk
International Political Science Association – http://www.ipsa.ca
National Council for Voluntary Organisations – http://
    www.ncvo-vol.org.uk

Political Studies Association, UK – http://www.psa.ac.uk

RDN Virtual Training Suite (internet tutorials) – http://www.rdn.ac.uk

Ringsurf (webrings) – http://www.ringsurf.com

Scottish Higher Education Funding Council – http://www.shefc.ac.uk

Shelter – http://england.shelter.org.uk/home/index.cfm

Stationery Office – http://www.the-stationery-office.co.uk

Student Loans Company – http://www.slc.co.uk

UCAS – http://www.ucas.ac.uk

University Association for Contemporary European Studies – http://www.uaces.org

Webring – http://dir.webring.com/rw

# Bibliography

Anderson, G. (1998) *Fundamentals of Educational Research*, 2nd edn, London: Falmer Press.

Basch, R. and Bates, E. (2000) *Researching Online for Dummies*, New York: IDG Books.

Bassey, M. (1999) *Case Study Research in Educational Settings*, Buckingham: Open University Press.

Battersby, M. (2000) *Using the Internet to Improve Teaching and Learning*, Northampton: Paragon.

Cameron, S. (2000) 'Evaluating Internet Sites for Academic Use: A Checklist for Students (and Teachers)', LTSN Briefing Paper 2. Available at http://hca.ltsn.ac.uk/resources/Briefing_Papers.php?who=bp2

Castells, M. (1997) *The Rise of Network Society 2: The Power of Identity*, Oxford: Blackwell.

Dawson, H. (2003) *Using the Internet for Political Research: Practical Hints and Tips*, Oxford: Chandos Publishing.

DeFleur, M. and Ball-Rokeach, S. (1982) *Theories of Mass Communication*, 4th edn, London: Longman.

Gates, W. (1995) *The Road Ahead*, London: Viking.

Golding, P. (2000) 'Information and Communications Technologies and the Sociology of the Future', *Sociology* 34 (1): 165–84.

Graham, D., McNeil, J. and Pettiford, L. (2000) *Untangled Web: Developing Teaching on the Internet*, Harlow: Prentice Hall.

Graham, G. (1999) *The Internet: A Philosophical Inquiry*, London: Routledge.

Gunter, B. (2000) *Media Research Methods: Measuring Audiences, Reactions and Impact*, London: Sage.

Hague, B. and Loader, B. (1999) *Digital Democracy: Discourse and Decision Making in the Information Age*, London: Routledge.

Harris, C. (1996) *An Internet Education. A Guide to Doing Research on the Internet*, Belmont, CA: Integrated Media Group.

Hewson, C., Yule, P., Laurent, D. and Vogel, C. (2003) *Internet Research Methods: A Practical Guide for the Social and Behavioural Sciences*, London: Sage.

Hill, K. and Hughes, J. (1998) *Cyberpolitics: Citizen Activism in the Age of the Internet*, London: Rowman and Littlefield.

Hine, C. (2000) *Virtual Ethnography*, London: Sage.

Holderness, M. (1998) *The Cyberspace Divide: Equality, Ageing and Policy in the Information Age*, London: Routledge.

Jolliffe, A., Ritter, J. and Stevens, D. (2001) *The Online Learning Handbook*, London: Kogan Page.

Jones, C. (1991) 'Qualitative Interviewing', in G. Allan and C. Skinner (eds), *Handbook for Research Students in the Social Sciences*, pp. 203–15, London: The Falmer Press.

Jones, S. (ed.) (1994) *Cybersociety*, New York: Sage.

Kolko, B., Nakamura, L. and Rodman, G. (eds) (2000) *Race in Cyberspace*, London: Routledge.

Lee, D. (2003) 'New Technologies in the Politics Classroom: Using Internet Classrooms to Support Teaching', *Politics* 23 (1): 66–73.

Lee, R. (2000) *Unobtrusive Methods in Social Research*, Buckingham: Open University Press.

Lewis, T. (1999) *Microsoft Rising and Other Tales of Silicon Valley*, Los Alamos, CA: IEEE Computer Systems Press.

Loader, R. (1997) *The Governance of Cyberspace: Politics, Technology and Global Restructuring*, London: Routledge.

Mann, C. and Stewart, F. (2000) *Internet Communication and Qualitative Research: A Handbook for Researching Online*, London: Sage.

Nickerson, R.S. (1994) 'Electronic Bulletin Boards: A Case Study of Computer-Mediated Communication', *Interacting with Computers* 6 (2): 117–34.

Oakley, A. (2000) Experiments *in Knowing: Gender and Method in the Social Sciences*, Oxford: Polity Press.

Ó Dochartaigh, N. (2002) *The Internet Research Handbook: A Practical Guide for Students and Researchers in the Social Sciences*, London: Sage.

Patton, M.Q. (1990) *Qualitative Evaluation and Research Methods*, 2nd edn, Newbury Park, CA: Sage.

Postmes, T., Spears, R. and Lea, M. (1998) 'Breaching or Building Social Boundaries?' *Communication Research* 25 (6): 689–715.

Powney, J. and Watts, M. (1987) *Interviewing in Educational Research*, London: Routledge & Kegan Paul.

Rash, W. (1997) *Politics on the Nets: Wiring the Political Process*, New York: W.H. Freeman.

Rheingold, H. (1993) *The Virtual Community: Homesteading in the Electronic Frontier*, Reading, MA: Addison-Wesley.

Rodrigues, D. and Rodrigues, R. (2000) *The Research Paper and the World Wide Web*, Upper Saddle River, NJ: Prentice Hall.

Schiller, D. (2000) *Digital Capitalism: Networking the Global Market System*, Cambridge, MA: MIT Press.

Schlein, A. (2002) *Find It Online: The Complete Guide to Online Research*, 3rd edn, Tempe, AZ: Facts on Demand Press.

Selwyn, N. and Robson, K. (1998) 'Using E-mail as a Research Tool', *Social Research Update*. Available at http://www.soc.surry.ac.uk/sru/SRU21.html [accessed on 02 February 2004].

Shea, V. (2002) 'Netiquette'. Available at http://www.albion.com/netiquette/book

Shenk, D. (1997) *Data Smog: Surviving the Information Glut*, New York: HarperCollins.

Shipman, M. (1997) *The Limitations of Social Research*, 4th edn, London: Longman.

Stein, S. (2000) *Learning on the Internet*, Harlow: Prentice Hall.

Stephenson, J. (ed.) (2001) *Teaching and Learning Online: Pedagogies for New Technologies*, London: Kogan Page.

Thomsen, S., Straubhar, J. and Bolyard, D. (1998) 'Ethnomethodology and the Study of Online Communities: Exploring the Cyber Streets', IRRIS 1998 Conference Paper. Available at http://www.sosig.ac.uk/iriss/papers/paper32.htm [accessed on 02 February 2004].

Toulouse, C. and Luke, T. (ed.) (1998) *The Politics of Cyberspace*, London: Routledge.

Turkle, S. (1997) *Life on the Screen: Identity in the Age of the Internet*, London: Phoenix.

Webster, F. (1996) *Theories of the Information Society*, London: Routledge.

White, J. (1999) *The Politico's Guide to Politics on the Internet*, London: Politico's Publishers.

Witmer, D.F., Colman, R.W. and Katzman, S.L. (1999) 'From Paper-and-Pencil to Screen-and-Keyboard: Toward a Methodology for Survey Research on the Internet,' in S. Jones (ed.) *Doing Internet Research. Critical Issues and Methods for Examining the Net*, pp. 145–63, London: Sage.

# Index